A Gri[illegible] for Modern Cunningfolk

Peter Paddon

A Grimoire for Modern Cunningfolk

Peter Paddon

PENDRAIG Publishing
Los Angeles, CA 91040

A Grimoire for Modern Cunningfolk
A Practical Guide to Witchcraft on the Crooked Path
by Peter Paddon
First Edition © 2011
Revised Edition © 2012
by PENDRAIG Publishing

Interior Images , Typeset & Layout Jo-Ann Byers Mierzwicki

PENDRAIG

PENDRAIG Publishing
Los Angeles, CA 91040
www.PendraigPublishing.com
Printed in the United States of America

ISBN: 978-0-9843302-1-8

Table of Contents

Introduction

A lot of things happened to me when I was seven. Among other things, I tranced out sitting cross-legged on the altar stone at Stonehenge, I heard the voice of (a) God call my name, like Samuel in the Old Testament, and I found out my father was a Witch. These all probably require a little explanation.

Stonehenge was local. The house I was born into was half a mile away from the ancient monument, though we moved about three miles further away when I was very little. Before the day of fences and no touching, we were actually taken to the stones as a school outing, to count and measure them. I worked through my worksheet really quickly, climbed up on the altar stone, and daydreamed for about half an hour before we were all bundled back into teachers' cars and driven back to school. To this day, I have no idea where I "went", except for a sense of being very far away.

The day I heard the Voice of God calling my name was a little more complex. It requires a little background. My father had certain interests that my mother greatly disapproved of, and in response to her demands of his "return to Christianity", he became a Mormon, taking the whole family with him. This irked my mother even more, because the Church wanted her to give up her precious tea. Anyway, despite the lower age limit of the Mormon priesthood being twelve, my father insisted on taking me with him to the priesthood meetings, and as he was not a well man, he taught me to do the healing by laying on of hands that the church taught, using his authority as a member of the priesthood, as I had none of my own — I was seven, after all. Anyway, all this gave me quite a lot of exposure to the Bible, and one day I was playing by the front door, and I heard a deep paternal voice say my name. Assuming it was my father, I bounced into the living room and asked my father why he called. He said he hadn't called. I went back to playing, and it happened again, with the same result. Then I caught on, remembering the story of Samuel in the Bible, I stood patiently waiting for the third time, but it never came. Not then, anyway.

Instead, my father started giving me snippets of what I later discovered were Witch Lore. My father and my mother had a falling out, and for a while my father moved out, until his worsening condition and another stroke caused my mother to take him back so she could look after him. While he was gone, though, she confided in me that he had been a member of a coven in Bristol, and while she thought he had joined the Mormons out of fear for his immortal soul, I later found out that he had actually joined to gain access to the esoteric teachings taught in the higher levels of the priesthood. My brother later confirmed this, adding that he had also been the member of a ceremonial magick lodge in Bristol (possibly the last of the original Golden Dawn lodges, which closed its doors for the last time in Bristol in 1976).

Fast-forward to the present day, and why I am writing this book. It is a while since I was seven, and in the intervening years I have disappointed my mother greatly by following in my father's footsteps. I left the Mormon Church pretty much the day my father died, and began to search for a coven or lodge who could teach me what I had glimpsed in my father's snippets. Along the way I took up with Madam Morgana, the White Witch of Buckinghamshire, trained with an Alexandrian coven in London and even ended up High Priest of my own coven, which slowly slid from orthodox

Alexandrian to something darker, more Shamanic, but still not what I was really looking for. I also joined the Rosicrucian's, the Builders of the Adytum, corresponded with the Servants of the Light and members of the OTO, and even started my own group working the Egyptian Mysteries. During this period I wrote my first two books, on Egyptian Ceremonial Magick, and became husband and father.

The marriage fell apart, and in an attempt to get away from bad memories, I visited the US, fell in love, and came back to get married. Almost as a reward for finding my soulmate, I found non-Wiccan Witchcraft, or rather it found me, as my new wife was a member of the coven I promptly trained and initiated with. Then, as that coven became less active, we were both introduced to another group, one that followed the Elder Faith and practiced the Nameless Art. We both realized we were home.

Now we are Magister and Mistress of our own coven, Briar Rose, and this book is an attempt to share what we have found in a meaningful way. Most books on witchcraft are about Wicca, which is a valid path, but not the only one, and usually from a fairly basic perspective. There are some excellent non-Wiccan books out there (Light From the Shadows by Gwyn, the works of Nigel Pennick and Nigel Jackson, the writings of Andrew Chumley), but they are hard to find unless you know they are there. I've been meaning to write more books ever since the first two, and in the last couple of years my series of spellcrafting DVDs (Craftwise) and my Crooked Path podcast have set the stage, so to speak. And my good friend Robin Artisson both encouraged me and led the way with his own books, the magnificent "Witching Way of the Hollow Hill", "The Horn of Evenwood" and "The Flaming Circle".

So here it is, A Grimoire for Modern Cunning Folk. I call it a grimoire because it is a workbook, an attempt to give you some of what you would find if you were a student in my coven, and I refer to us as Modern Cunning Folk because the reclaiming of the word Witch has entered very surreal territory these days. The people who taught the people who taught me never used the word witch except in a derogatory sense, so even though technically it is an accurate term to use, I try to steer clear of it, and the term Cunning Man or Cunning Woman is also moderately accurate, without any "mystical" baggage that will make people want to claim it as anything other than what it is.

I should point out that this entire book is based on my own personal Path. I work with a group, Briar Rose, and that group has a specific way of doing things that is informed by the work we have done together and what we have learnt from other sources. As Magister, obviously the group's work and my own work are very closely aligned, but the nature of this book necessitates that it tells a very personal story — within its pages I am recounting my understanding of that Path, and because I have my own pet theories and bias, that is not going to be exactly the same book that another member of Briar Rose would write.

Originally, this was going to be as generic a book as I could write, and in some respects, it still is. But the qualifier of "as generic as possible" turned out to be "not very". So despite my original intent, I have elected to include the deities and some of the other entities that we work with, as an example. But just because we work with the Lore and Mysteries of Celtic Wales (specifically those found in the Mabinogion) does not mean that you can't work this Path with different myths, different Gods. Essentially, this will work within the framework of any religious practice (if somewhat heretically in some cases), mine just happens to be Welsh.

The book you hold is a thank you to my father, for planting the seeds, to Nigel and Seldiy, who taught me the basics of ritual so well, and to those who taught me to walk the Crooked Path. It is an account of my Path, my beliefs, and my practices — I make no claims of lineage or authority for what is given here. Judge it purely by how effective it is for you, for in the end, that matters more than how many generations have said the words and mixed the herbs before you. There is a current that sustains and informs this work, but it may not be the current that is important for you — but the practice is valid whatever the current, so I present the practice here in the hopes that it will enable you to immerse yourself in the current of your own Path.

Bendith,
Peter Paddon,
Magister of Coven Briar Rose.

The Cunning Art

Witchcraft in the British Isles has been called many things; the Old Persuasion, the Art, the Craft, the Nameless Art and the Cunning Art, to name just a few. Most are self explanatory, but the Cunning Art deserves a closer look. The word Cunning comes from the Anglo-Saxon "kennen", to know, and it makes an appearance in another phrase often associated with Witches, wort-cunning (herb knowledge). So from this, it is easy to see that the Cunning Art is a path of gnosis, or knowledge. As it was written over the entrance to the Temple of the Mysteries, "know Thyself."

As an esoteric path, the Cunning Art is a journey of self discovery. Although much is taught through the use of myth and Lore, the emphasis is on personal experience. We examine the old stories, or myths, and extract Lore from them, from which we construct exercises and rituals in order to experience the core of the myth and the Lore. We firmly believe in the process of leading students to discover key wisdom for themselves, so that they can own the knowledge and not have to take it on faith. This is perhaps the most significant factor of this path, and it can be very frustrating for the students — we often answer a question with another question, and we talk in riddles, poems, and will push our students to come up with the answers to their own questions. This process requires students to be able to make critical analysis and to think for themselves, and this has become much harder since schools and universities have abandoned this way of learning.

Another key feature of the Cunning Art is the emphasis that is placed on working with Ancestors, which is a good indication of the shamanic nature of the path. Modern practice is concerned with enfleshing Lore passed down from our ancestors, and recovering Lore that has been lost, using practices that are collectively known as "tapping the bone". In the context of this art, the term Ancestor refers to both our genetic and spiritual forebears, and because we believe time to be non-linear, we refer to "ancestor long gone, and ancestors yet to be". When we talk about the Ancestors, we often use the term "River of Blood" in the sense of a bloodline, and also the "Bone Ladder". These are in other Traditions sometimes referred to as the Red Thread, the Ancestral lineage that defines a Tradition. Being somewhat anarchic as Cunning Folk should be, we prefer to think of lineage as something that is only relevant — if at all — within a particular group. For us the emphasis is on the individual forging their own link with the Ancestors, so they do not have to rely on a hierarchy or lineage to validate them.

This is not a path of reconstruction, and although my group works with the Welsh deities, we are not Celtic Reconstructionists. Rather, we attempt to create something that works for us, whether it includes practices from our ancient Ancestors or totally new ones, without fear or favour. So you won't find us revealing secrets of how the Ancient Celts worked with their deities, because, no matter how fond we are of all things Celtic, we are not attempting to revert to a past that is known only through speculation. Instead, we follow the clues in our Lore, and the results of experiments and conversations with the Ancestors, to forge a practice that is relevant to us, here and now.

I should probably point out that technically and historically, the term Cunning Man refers to a solitary practitioner who earns a living by working spells for the local community, for fertility, good fortune, healing, etc. Some were snake oil salesmen, or con men, and some were genuine practitioners, but none claimed to be Witches, and in fact most were church-going Christians. My use of the term Cunning Folk does not imply that they are the same as what we are trying to be, because that is not so. But the spirit of what they were, the independent search for wisdom and true practice — regardless of the religious persuasion — is at the core of what modern Cunning Folk are trying to construct. I do not consider what we do to be reconstruction, because we are not trying to recreate the practices of times gone by, but rather to create Lore and Practice that draws upon the deep well of Ancestral Memory in a way that gives us tools that are valid today.

Gods and Archetypes on the Crooked Path

It is important to remember that the Crooked Path can be walked in the shadow of any religion or spirituality, or none at all, for that matter. The Gods encountered upon that Path are very likely to be strongly influenced by the God or Gods of the religion practiced, but there are certain archetypes that are embodied for the modern Crafter that are universal.

There is quite a difference in opinion among various Pagans as to the nature of deity. For some, they are living, breathing entities in their own right, while others see them as archetypes, or representations of deep-seated facets of our own psyche. The whole argument of whether they come from within or without is debated fiercely and eternally on various internet forums, but ultimately the only opinion that matters is your own, formulated from your own experience. For myself, I always answer "both", not only because there are differences in the nature of different deities, but because I believe — based on my own subjective experience and interaction with the Gods and Goddesses I work with — that they truly do partake of both.

The Horned Lord, or "Auld Hornie"

Also known as the Horned Master, this is the archetypical God of the Witches, and can be embodied by the All-Father, Odin, Herne, Cernunnos, Gwynn, and other similar deities. He is often portrayed as the Master Magician, a Trickster who teaches us by putting us through experiences. There are strong influences of the Underworld, as well as the Wild Man of the Forest, and He almost seems to be using His human visage as a mask for something older, deeper and darker. In Scottish Witchcraft, he would be unashamedly referred to as "the De'il", and he certainly plays the role of the Devil in the pre-Christian sense — the adversary who provides the momentum and motivation to move through the experience and achieve the goal. In this way, he is the Devil wrestled in the churchyard for the Toad Bone, the Black Man at the Crossroads who grants us our greatest desire, the Trickster who fools us into thinking the Path of Fate we walk is one we "chose".

My own experiences with Auld Hornie have almost always been in the guise of Herne, and some of them have been alarmingly "real world". I remember walking in Salsey Forest (between Milton Keynes and Northampton in England), and being aware of the sound of a stag walking parallel with me but several feet away, hidden by dense trees and undergrowth. I kept going, looking for a gap, and eventually found one, only to find no sign of the stag except hoof prints astride a fallen branch that made a perfect staff for me.

My second experience was in woodland near Woburn Abbey. It was Yule Eve, and we were gathering holly to decorate the altar for the next night's ritual, when I saw a white stag running through the trees. But the third encounter was the most profound for me. It was the early hours of Christmas Day, just before dawn, and I had lost my way going home from a gig at a restaurant in London, and had ended up in Windsor Royal Park somehow. The light was that funny pre-dawn grey, compounded by a fog that hung low on the ground, and I parked my car to stretch my legs and get some fresh air, seeing what looked like a huge oak tree looming out of the mist. I decided to walk over to it, and as I did, I heard the baying of hounds, and then the sound of horses' hooves, and from behind me a horned rider and his dogs swept past me and the tree, fading quickly into the mist. Despite the physicality of all of it, there was an otherworldly quality that told me they were not mundane, and on returning home it was not a great surprise to read that there was once a royal huntsman called Herne, who hanged himself on the Great Royal Oak in Windsor Royal Park, who became associated with Herne the deity, and that there were many accounts of people seeing the Wild Hunt by that tree.

Le Grand Belle Dame Sans Merci, or The White Lady

Often referred to as the Queen of Fate, she is frequently mistaken for the Great Mother of nature-based religions, but she is not a nature or fertility Goddess, but rather the Mistress of the Mysteries. Cold and aloof, she nevertheless brings us what we need on the Path, and is often embodied by such Goddesses as Goda. In Briar Rose we rarely call upon Her, but She will make Her presence known when there is a need, and She is always present at our initiations.

The Black Goddess, or Dark Mother

It is said that the Dark Mother exists outside the Wheel of Manifestation. In the Great Stone Circle of existence, she is the heelstone that stands beyond, to the North East. She is the fixed point to which we apply the lever of our will in order to move the Universe and bring about Change. Some would say that she is embodied by such as Cerridwen or the Mill Wife, and there is certainly value in exploring that, but it is wise not to let that become an assumed truth, because there is far more to this enigmatic Lady than that.

Encountering the Black Goddess is an essential part of your Path if you wish to master the Cunning Arts rather than just be a journeyman, but it is not an easy or enjoyable experience in most cases. Nothing can prepare you for the way She turns your life upside down, but by the same token, there is no substitute for the total transformation She brings about. I will write more about this in the section on the Nightmares of Lilith, later in the book.

The Lord and Lady

Here we come to a more familiar place for those who started out in Wicca. The Lord and Lady here can be embodied by the Gods and Goddesses of Nature, or by the Faery Court. It is the Lord who is manifest in the Wheel of the Year as Sacred King, and the Lady who is His Consort. He goes through the metamorphosis from Child of Promise, through Warrior, Lover, Priest and King, to the Wraith form of the Dragon Beneath the mound. Each year at Midwinter he is born of the Dark Mother's barren cauldron in wraith form, to be brought to manifestation as the Child of Promise by the Maid, brought into manhood by the Mother, sacrificed by the Crone, and reborn by the Queen.

Even in my Wiccan days, I used a vision quest technique to go and talk with the Lord and Lady, and found to my surprise that few of the other Wiccans I knew ever did that. They would draw down the Moon and the Sun in circle, invoking the God and Goddess to empower their rites, but never seemed to go and talk to them. I remember sharing my technique with a Witch from Aberdeen, and the tears running down her cheeks as she talked about how she had never had an experience like that in all her years of the Craft. For that reason, I give the exercise in the form of a pathworking here.

Encountering the Lord and Lady

Start by using any relaxation technique you like, and sit with your eyes closed. Make sure your arms and legs are not crossed, and take three deep breaths. With each breath, feel the stress and tension of the day fading away, being replaced with a calm expectation. Continue to breathe deeply, as your journey begins.

See before you a pair of pillars, with a midnight blue curtain suspended between them. You part the curtains and see a grey mist beyond, but right in the centre of your vision is a silver star, floating without support. You examine the star, noticing how clear and "present" it is, but suddenly, without warning, the star disappears. You find yourself pulled into the space where it was, passing through the pillars and into the mist. Everything goes grey as you feel yourself lifted up, floating up and away, eventually drifting down, to find your feet landing on a grassy hill, as the mist clears. You find yourself on a hilltop, looking down onto woodland in the valley below, a narrow dirt path leads down the hillside to the edge of the forest, and you begin to follow it, feeling a breeze in the air as you descend.

Entering the forest, the path continues along, winding between the trees, and you follow it in the dappled green light that filters through the leaves. You hear the rustling of creatures in the undergrowth, but do not see any of the animals as you follow the crooked path deeper and deeper into the forest.

Ahead you notice that there is a fork in the path, and you pause, pondering which fork to take. Suddenly you see a flash of white further along one of the paths, and this is the path you choose, walking rapidly along, trying to see what the white flash was. Turning a bend in the path, you see a white stag a short way ahead, looking back as if to check that you are following, before it heads off down the path again. You follow, unable to catch up, but avoiding being left behind, as the path continues to twist and turn between the trees.

Deep in the heart of the forest now, the canopy is thick and the dim green filtered sunlight serves only to accentuate the shadows, so it is with some surprise that you turn a bend in the path to find yourself breaking out into a clearing at the heart of the forest. In the centre of the clearing is a fountain, encircled by rocks about the right side to sit on, and the tranquil atmosphere along with the gentle tinkling of the water draws you to go and sit by the fountain.

Sitting in contemplation, you hear a sound like a church bell ringing in the distance, and you look up in the direction it came from, to see a beautiful woman entering the clearing. Naked and tanned, with long flowing hair, she is the most beautiful woman you have ever seen, and you watch, captivated, as she walks across the clearing to come and sit by the fountain across from you. Her eyes are filled with joy, and a smile forms on her face as she regards you.

Then another sound breaks the silence — a hunting horn. Looking up in the direction this new sound came from, you see another form enter the clearing. This time it is a handsome man, muscular, tanned and equally as naked as the Lady who now sits with you. As he walks towards you, there is a grin on his face and mischief in his eyes, but you hardly notice because you cannot take your eyes off the magnificent antlers growing out of his head. He too comes and sits beside the fountain, next to the Lady, and beckons you to speak with them.

(Pause)

Once your conversation is at an end, thank the Lord and Lady, and ask them if you might return again. Then say your farewells and turn to cross the clearing to the path that brought you here. As you turn, you see that while you were talking, the animals from the forest have come into the clearing, and are waiting patiently for the Lord and Lady.

With one last look over your shoulder at the pair, you re-enter the forest, and follow the twisting path back to the fork, where you pick up the original trail that leads to the hilltop. You quickly make your way to the edge of the forest, returning to the hilltop, where the mist once more envelops you and you feel yourself lifted up and back, until your feet come to rest once again at the two pillars. You walk back between the pillars, as the curtain closes behind you. Contemplating your journey for a moment, you then turn your attention to your physical surroundings as you open your eyes, and the journey is over.

Notable Points on the Path of the King

Everything hangs on the Wheel. Well, as in most things esoteric, there is more to that statement than meets the eye, but it is true that in this path, the Wheel of the Year creates a powerful framework on which to hang Lore, practice and ritual in a way that ties everything together. For us, the cycle of Festivals laid out around the Wheel of the Year embody the journey of the King, and our seasonal rituals are all about enacting these Mysteries rather than the agricultural celebrations found in Wicca. For simplicity, I have included the eight Sabbats that are familiar from Wiccan Lore and literature. Some traditional Crafters — including us — use them, others do not. But they are a good balanced starting point. You might want to eventually add to them (we did), or replace them altogether, but they are perfectly fine as a starting point.

So who is this King? Well he is the Sacred King, the Hero of Myth and Lore, often personified as a slain and risen God like Llew, Osiris or Jesus. We tend to work primarily with Welsh Celtic deities; so much of our Wheel work revolves around aspects of the story of

Llew, although it applies also to Math, Son of Mathonwy, Mabon, Son of Modron, and many other heroes. I have a personal bias, as Llew is my Patron, but I try to be fair to the others. It is important to note that while the term King is a masculine title, and many of the heroes of these stories are male, the Mysteries themselves are not gendered, and can be enacted or worked by either sex. We sometimes look to myths that have a female protagonist to make this clearer, but in truth the important polarity in the myths is that of initiator and facilitator, rather than male and female.

We have used the Sacred King cycle in several different ways, by having a person "carry" Sacred King for the coven through an entire year, having a male and female "Jack and Jill" work the cycle together, and with everyone being their own personal Sacred King. We have also run through a couple of years with a different person as Sacred King for each Sabbat. Each version has its pros and cons.

Carrying Sacred King on behalf of the coven is a very profound experience for the individual, but it does tend to relegate the other coveners to the role of spectator, though they can still get deep insights if they make the effort. In an ideal world, everyone would get to take their turn at it, but in a larger group that entails waiting several years for your "turn". Using the "Jack and Jill" model (yes, named after the nursery rhyme characters) speeds up the process as well as exposing the Initiator/Initiatee relationship nicely, but it is a very different cycle because the focus has changed. Letting everyone be their own Sacred King keeps everyone involved, but the focus is on the personal path then, rather than the shared Lore and egregore of the coven. We have found that changing it up between all of the methods to be most effective, because it enables us to use what is appropriate for the dynamics of the group, the specific time period and the wider world.

I was lucky enough to walk the Wheel as Sacred King for my coven the year after I was initiated into the Crooked Path, and it is an experience that I cherish, even though it has to be said that this particular journey is not an easy one to make. My "reign" started with the coven Mistress announcing at the end of the Yule celebration that I would be Sacred King for the coming year.

Imbolc or Candlemas

Most accounts of the Wheel of the Year start with Imbolc or with Yule, and this one is no exception, but it is not an easy place to start. You really have to understand that our Wheel considers the period between Samhain and Imbolc to be the Dark Time, when the Horned Lord is beyond the Veil of the mound and is essentially inaccessible to us. At Imbolc, the Horned Lord is made manifest in the form of the Child of Promise, and the manifestation is the work of the Maid, bringing Him forth from the Cauldron. This is not to be confused with a birth, despite the cauldron-womb connection — note it is the Maid, not the Mother that brings Him forth. He enters manifestation from the Cauldron-as-Mound/Tomb rather than the Cauldron-as-Womb.

The Child of Promise is, of course, each one of us, and the manifestation within us is represented by the lighting of a candle, symbolizing the flame at our heart/hearth.

My year of carrying Sacred King really began with the Imbolc rite, where I played the role of the Child of Promise. After the Child was invoked or made manifest within me while I stood in the cauldron, I got to light each person's candle and speak to them from the heart, awakening each one's own Child of Promise within. It was a gentle start to the year, yet one that moved me deeply, as I felt myself planted firmly in place on the Wheel of the Year. It started as a gentle ride, but quickly became more like the experience of Jack Sparrow in Pirates of the Caribbean: Dead Man's Chest, where he, William Turner and the former Commodore are fighting on the runaway water wheel. I guess it was all a matter of momentum...

Spring Equinox

In the story of Llew, his mother, Arianrhod, lays a geas upon Him that He will not receive a name or arms from anyone but her, and it is through the trickery of Gwydion that He attains his rite of passage into manhood. At Spring Equinox, we work the Mystery of Coming of Age, where the Hero is named and armed, and sent out into exile to seek His Fate. This can be expressed in several ways, through the walking of the shepherd's Race and receiving the Gifts of Arianrhod at the centre of the maze, or through encountering Nectan at the Well, in order to receive a blessing on the start of your quest, as the Knights received purification and sanctification from him before setting off to find the Grail.

The working can also manifest in a very emotional way. For several years, initiates of our Path referred to Spring Equinox as the "fuck you" rite, because the impetus for the exile manifested as a rebellion against authority. I'm pleased to say that, valuable though the experience was, the Mystery seems to have settled on a more benign manifestation in recent years, becoming more of a communion with the initiate's Patron or Matron.

My experience of this Sabbat as Sacred King is a little hazy. It was one of those "fuck you" years, and I was exiled from the circle top find my/the King's Path after being named and armed. I remember passing through forest, despite the covenstead being in the middle of urban North Hollywood, and by all accounts it took them some time to find me afterwards, despite the fact I was sitting on a couch in the next room — they kept looking in there, but did not see me until my perception returned to the mundane.

Beltaine, or May Eve

This is the festival where we work the Mystery of the Sacred Marriage, the Hieros Gamos. Our hero, having attained manhood, now fulfils his desire by uniting with the Maid. In the process, He transforms Her into the Mother, ensuring the continuation of the Cycle. In many ways, it is the Maid who undergoes initiation this time, facilitated by the King/Hero. Sometimes this rite can express itself through a sexual union, but this is not essential, as the true Hieros Gamos is the union of the Lower and Higher selves within the mundane form of the Initiate. In our path, we refer to this as the union of the Drake and Crown.

As Sacred King I had the unique experience of consummating the Hieros Gamos with the May Queen fully and completely, just not physically. Simultaneously deeply erotic and profoundly spiritual, it is hard to describe in anything but sensual terms, even though it by far transcended a merely sexual act. It was at this point where it became apparent that the journey was not going to be one of love and light, as the insights I gained foreshadowed the darker rites to come.

Midsummer

For the Sacred King, the Midsummer rite is a time of sacrifice, as He is literally "made sacred" in order to become Priest to His people. The fulfilment of desire behind Him, He lays down His personal desires for the good of the tribe, and makes His future decisions based on what is good for the tribe, rather than for His own personal needs and wants.

The laying down of desire is represented by His symbolic castration, which in turn is represented by the cutting of mistletoe from His body, to be hung on the Bile Tree until Midwinter. Strangely enough, this ritual is always very potent for everyone who participates, and each year when we sit down to plan the coming rite, it is almost impossible to remember what we did in previous years. It is almost as if this rite has to be completely 'new' each year.

True to the years before and since, the Midsummer rite of my year as Sacred King is definitely a little blurry. About the only thing I truly remember is the symbolic castration, performed by lopping mistletoe hanging between my thighs with a sharp sickle. I'm told that the priestess carrying the Mother came close to making it non-symbolic, but either way, I think I would have been okay with either outcome, because I was so in the moment.

When we have an individual carrying Sacred King, it is usual for that person to be completely celibate between Midsummer and Lammas, honouring the spirit of the act of symbolic castration. For me this resulted in a deeply sensual encounter with the Pale Lady, resulting in several ecstatic nocturnal experiences where she brought me to powerful and extended orgasms with no physical interaction on anyone's behalf, knocking me out of my physical body with the force of the release and taking me to place that, even now, I have trouble finding the words to describe.

Lammas

A harvest festival with a difference, the Hero makes the ultimate sacrifice, and offers Himself up to Fate, hanging on the Tree, just as Llew — in the form of an eagle — took refuge in a tree after being speared by Geronwy, the lover of Blodwedd. In our rite, the Sacred King is offered up as a sacrifice along with a scapegoat, a loaf of bread. The working involves senior initiates literally hanging on the Bile Tree by their initiate cords, and taking a journey with the Sacred King into the Underworld. The whole thing is presided over by the Mill-wife, a form of the Dame, and upon the acceptance of the scapegoat loaf, the King returns to be crowned. Although rare, it has happened that the Sacred King has been taken instead of the scapegoat (i.e., the person representing the King dies at this time of year), in which case the coven immediately goes into Dark Time as if it were Samhain. In one case, an initiate who knew he was dying took the role of sacred King in order to make his passing more meaningful to himself and those he loved, and did indeed pass around this time of year. To quote a phrase written about another Sacred King, "Greater love hath no man than this…" It is at Lammas that the Mother becomes the Crone.

What can I say about hanging on the Tree? As Sacred King, I experienced a journey through the Underworld, passing through three sets of great gates (one bronze, one silver, one gold), that took me to the Great Enclosure at the centre of the Earth, where I came face to face with the Black Interior Sun, and embraced my Fate by leaping into it and surrendering myself to the certainty that I was not going to return from this journey. It was not until I acknowledged and fully accepted the fact that I was going to die that I was released from its grasp and was allowed to ascend back up to where my body and the rest of the coven were. I'm told that when they all got back up I was not breathing and there was a tense minute or two before I drew a breath and returned to them. What I do know for sure is that although I returned, part of me stayed with the Interior Sun, and remains there to this day. Because of that I can take myself back there in an instant, which is extremely useful for the crafting I do, and this was the start of the journey that led to my discovery of the visceral nature of magick.

Autumn Equinox

At Autumn Equinox, the exiled Hero returns to His tribe as Priest-King, to lead them in renewing their commitment to the Hearth and the Heart of the Mysteries. At this point the Red River of Blood and the white Celestial River of the Milky Way are joined by the Bone Ladder. Vows are re-affirmed, and the tribe or family is strengthened.

Almost every year we take our cauldron, hearthstone and ancestral skull to the ocean, to wash and cleanse them under the moonlight with meditation and chanting before we gather round the ancient stone to renew our commitment to the Mysteries and to each other.

In many ways, this is the simplest and easiest rite for one who carries Sacred King, because the role of the King is passive. It is, however, deeply moving and emotional, to blood the hearth stone and reaffirm the vows as the Sacred King.

Samhain, or Hallows

At Samhain the cauldron is overturned as the womb becomes the tomb, and the Sacred King enters the mound and passes beyond the Veil as Dark Time fall upon us. This Mystery of Death and what lies beyond is worked alongside the more public Mystery of the Wild Hunt, where Gwyn ap Nudd gathers the souls of those who have died during the year and takes them into the Mound to enter Cerridwen's Cauldron of Rebirth. From this rite until the Rite of Imbolc, no male deity is called on. The Crone, having assisted the Lord into the Mound and keened at His passing, becomes the Queen.

Our rite includes separating the Sacred King from the one carrying it, so he can enter the Mound as our divine messenger to the Gods, while the person who carried him is released so that they don't follow him across that threshold, never to return. From this point on, the title of Sacred King is symbolic only for the person who carried it. In recent years we have passed the mantle of Sacred King to a giant poppet filled with straw, which is wrapped in the altar cloth and cremated at the end of the rite.

Yule

At the point of Midwinter, the Queen of Fate gives birth to the Horned Lord — in Wraith form — from the cauldron. Although reborn, the Hero is not yet made manifest. For that He must wait for Imbolc.

As you can see, there are definite links to the agricultural cycle practiced by the various Folk religions revived under the umbrella of neo-Paganism, but these underlying Mysteries are in fact all part of one Greater Mystery known as the Path of the Fool, or the Hero or sacred King. It is a cycle that profoundly affects each and every person working the Tradition, and is one of the key things that draws people to this path. There are other sabbats that we work as well as these, but that can wait for later — I'm a firm believer in taking things in bite-sized chunks.

With the birth of the Wraith Lord, the one who carried Sacred King for the year is released, which considering the events of the year, turned out to be a bittersweet moment for me. A great weight was lifted from me, while at the same time I knew I had been transformed in ways that would continue to take me by surprise for years to come.

The Seeking Guardians of Lore

Closely related to the wheel of the Year is the Compass Round. This is another construct on which we can hang Myth and Lore, and the one can be overlaid over the other. But the Compass isn't just a construct, it is also a concept, because when we refer to the Compass of the Circle, we are also referring to our personal ethical compass, and this is a key part of our practice and beliefs. Where a Wiccan might cast a circle in which to work and celebrate, we generally lay a Compass. It is essentially the same thing in practice, but the intent, symbolism and technique are all quite different.

As a construct, the Compass contains the layout of our ritual space. At the Quarter we have Guardians, deities who we work with placed at key points to provide access to the Inner Realms and their Lore. These deities are not fixed in place, but are rather called in specific locations as an aid to memory, and to invoke certain relationships — they are free to move where they will within the Sacred space. This construct is purely for our convenience, and as a teaching and working tool it is very effective for us. Other non-wiccan Traditions use similar constructs, though the details are likely to be different.

There are several layers to the Compass construct, the first being the Quarter Gates and their Guardians. It is important to note that while I give as examples the deities we use as Guardians, it is more important to work with deities or forms that are relevant to you, so you should not blindly follow any examples as if they were holy writ.

East

In Northern Quarters the Gates are known by the Airts, or qualities of light. These can be named as Earth, Air, Fire and Water, but they are not the classical Elements as used by the Golden Dawn and most forms of Wicca. For that reason, while the above names are perfectly valid, we use names that are more in tune with the essence of the Airts, and so the East is the Gate of the Sun.

This is the place of dawn, of the first warm stirrings of daylight, and the lighting of the fire in the hearth, perhaps lit by the embers left from the previous day. Most books will refer to this gate as Fire, but it is the literal flame of the hearth-fire or forge fire rather than the Element of Transformation.

The deities who guard this gate will be gods of Light (note, not necessarily solar deities). Llew/Lugh is often mistaken for a Solar deity, but He is in fact a God of Light, not the Sun, and as a Light-Bringer He has obvious associations with the Morning Star, Venus, and Lucifer. It is interesting to note that in the Bible, Jesus is referred to as the Bright and Morning Star.

In addition to Gods of Light, Forge Gods may be found guarding this gate. As there will often be a God and a Goddess acting as guardians, it is not uncommon to find Traditions that make use of an often forgotten aspect of Bridhe as the Forge Maiden. This is most obvious in the Welsh regional version of Bridhe, Fraidd.

You've probably noticed that the God and Goddess given here are not a "couple", husband and wife. This is because the emphasis is not on fertility rites, but on the Mysteries of Initiation. We work with Llew in part because He is our prime example of the cycle of the Sacred King, but also because he brings in many of the creative aspects of enlightenment. The Forge Goddess, Fraidd, is also quite obviously connected to creativity, and between them they represent a very practical kind of wisdom and understanding that is key to our Mysteries and our Path as a whole.

Through the Gate of the Sun

Make sure you are sitting comfortably, with your eyes closed, and relax your body. Start with your left leg, tighten the muscles and then relax them. Then the right leg — tighten the muscles there, relax them, and let them go completely. Then your abdomen and stomach tighten the muscles up and then release them, let them go completely.

Now your chest and breathing muscles tighten them up and then relax them. Your back, shoulder, and neck muscles, tighten them up as tight as they'll go and as you release them feel the tension of the day just draining away. It's a wonderful feeling. Now your head and face muscles tighten them up as tight as they'll go. Tighten them up as tight as they'll go and then relax them. Lastly, do the muscles of your arms. Tighten them up as tight as they'll go and then relax them, from the shoulders down to the finger tips.

Now become aware of the black nothingness around you. Feel yourself floating, and then moving forward, lifting, drifting away. As you feel yourself floating away, the blackness fades to grey, becoming like a foggy mist as you begin to descend.

Your feet make contact with a surface, and you find yourself sitting in a small round boat — a coracle — which is floating through the mist on a river. It gently moves towards a bank, and comes to a halt, and you climb out and onto the riverbank.

The riverbank is forested, but where you climbed out of the coracle there is a pathway leading into the forest, and you follow it. The path is narrow, and twists and turns through the trees as it takes you deep into the heart of the forest.

You notice the sound of metal on metal, in a rhythmic hammering, and follow the sound as the path brings you to a clearing in the forest. In the clearing you see the back of a simple hut, set up as a blacksmith's workshop. The sound of hammering is coming from the other side of the hut, so you walk round, to see a woman of average build, dark-haired, wielding a hammer as she shapes the hot metal upon the anvil. Beside her, the glowing coals of the forge radiate heat. This is Fraidd, the Forge Maiden. Moving round, you approach her and she pauses in her work, regarding you with an appraising eye...

(Pause for conversation with Fraidd)

You realize that the minutes have passed quickly, and it is time to move on. Making your farewells to Fraidd, you move to the far side of the clearing.

You set off on the path that leads on from the clearing, a wider, straighter path that keeps the sky visible above. Before you know it, you find yourself approaching a stone building nestled among the trees. It is a hunting lodge, and its doors are open, so you enter, noting the array of animal trophies and weapons decorating the wall. A short hall leads you to a doorway, and inside is a room that has a black floor and a fireplace at the far end. Standing before the fire-place, with his back to you, is a tall slim male wearing a red tunic and black pants, who has flowing brown hair, almost like a lion's mane. As you walk towards him, you realize that there appears to be stars reflected in the floor, even though the room has a simple white ceiling. The man turns to greet you, his extended hands are the work-worn hands of a craftsman, despite his noble bearing. This is Llew, Master Crafter and warrior...

(Pause for conversation with Llew)

Once again, it is time to move on, and you thank Llew before leaving the building to continue your journey.

This time the path leading away from the clearing curves sinuously this way and that, in great lazy loops, until before you know it, you find yourself at the riverbank again. Although this is much further downstream, the coracle has floated down this far and is waiting for you. Carefully, you climb into it once more, and no sooner are you seated than it begins to move away from the bank, taking you into the mist, which gets thicker and thicker, until all you can see is the coracle. Soon the mist closes in completely, leaving you in a featureless grey expanse as you feel yourself floating up and back.

The grey mist fades to black, and you feel yourself returning to the place you started from, sitting with your eyes closed. Sit up and open your eyes. The journey is over.

South

The Southern Airt is the Gate of Stone. This is the place of noon, when the sun is highest in the sky and everything is at its most lively. The warmth of day has released the fragrances of the plants, and on days that are warm enough, the loamy scent of the earth itself is carried on the air.

The deities who guard this gate will be closely associated with nature. Earth Mother Goddesses are appropriate here, especially those who invoke the rich musk and fertility of the soil. Modron from the Welsh pantheon, or Gaia for a more generic touch, fits the bill perfectly here.

The male deities are often more oriented toward animals rather than plants — still wild and untamed, but ready to run with the herd, and rut. Herne and Pan, or their more "civilized" brother Cernunnos, are apt guardians here. We work with Herne here, more British than Welsh, though Gwyn ap Nudd would not be inappropriate.

Through the Gate of the Stone

Make sure you are sitting comfortably, with your eyes closed, and relax your body. Start with your left leg, tighten the muscles and then relax them. Then the right leg — tighten the muscles there, relax them, and let them go completely. Then your abdomen and stomach tighten the muscles up and then release them, let them go completely.

Now your chest and breathing muscles tighten them up and then relax them. Your back, shoulder, and neck muscles, tighten them up as tight as they'll go and as you release them feel the tension of the day just draining away. It's a wonderful feeling. Now your head and face muscles tighten them up as tight as they'll go. Tighten them up as tight as they'll go and then relax them. Lastly, do the muscles of your arms. Tighten them up as tight as they'll go and then relax them, from the shoulders down to the finger tips.

Now become aware of the black nothingness around you. Feel yourself floating, and then moving forward, lifting, drifting away. As you feel yourself floating away, the blackness fades to grey, becoming like a foggy mist as you begin to descend.

Your feet make contact with a surface, and you find yourself sitting in a small round boat — a coracle — which is floating through the mist on a river. It gently moves towards a bank, and comes to a halt, and you climb out and onto the riverbank.

The riverbank is forested, but where you climbed out of the coracle there is a pathway leading into the forest, and you follow it. The path is narrow, and twists and turns through the trees as it takes you deep into the heart of the forest, eventually coming to a shady clearing, still covered high above by the green canopy provided by the tall trees around it.

In the centre of the clearing is a mound, green with moss and plants, but clearly made from three great stones supporting a huge slab of granite, covered now by dirt and undergrowth. You hear a sound like deep sighs from within, and find your way through the growth covering the stones, to enter the mound.

Inside it is surprisingly warm, and a little humid. It is difficult to see in what little light makes it into the mound, but the texture of the rock under your fingers feels like it has been carved with intricate maze symbols and spirals. You become aware of a presence in the centre of this place, and as your eyes adjust to the dim light, you see the matronly form of Modron, planted firmly in the ground…

(pause for conversation with Modron)

Almost before you get going, it seems that is time for you to continue your journey. Promising Modron that you will return again, you make your farewells, and wriggle out of the mound once more.

You set off on the path that leads on from the clearing, a wider, straighter path that keeps the sky visible above. Before you know it, you find yourself approaching a small hill that appears to be more or less a large rock jutting out of the ground. You climb up the rocky surface, which takes you up above the treetops and into the sunlight.

Standing at the highest point, looking out over the forest, you see the muscular back of a man, tanned, naked, and rippling with power. But all of this fades into insignificance as you notice the fine antlers that extend from either side of his head. He turns, with a smile on his face and a glint in his eye, and you find yourself face to face with Herne…

(pause for conversation with Herne)

Once again, the need to continue your journey catches up with you. Surprised to see that the sun is beginning to set, you thank Herne and continue on your way.

This time the path leading away from the clearing curves sinuously this way and that, in great lazy loops, until before you know it, you find yourself at the riverbank again. Although this is much further downstream, the coracle has floated down this far and is waiting for you. Carefully, you climb into it once more, and no sooner are you seated than it begins to move away from the bank, taking you into the mist, which gets thicker and thicker, until all you can see is the coracle. Soon the mist closes in completely, leaving you in a featureless grey expanse as you feel yourself floating up and back.

The grey mist fades to black, and you feel yourself returning to the place you started from, sitting with your eyes closed. Sit up and open your eyes. The journey is over.

West

The western Airt is the Gate of the Sea. This is the threshold place of disk, when the veil is thin between the realms and seers see, and Crafters craft. To stand at the crossroads, or with one foot on land and the other in the ocean, both under a grey sky, is to stand where magick is truly worked.

The deities who guard this gate are water Gods, though not necessarily Gods of the Sea. River, lake and weather deities can guard this place as well, so you may find Manannan, Welsh God of the Sea, or his more elusive cousin, Nudd, associated with water wherever it is found.

Goddesses too, may be associated with water through their tales, rather than being specific sea deities. Cerridwen, keeper of the Cauldron of Rebirth, and strongly associated with Lake Bala in Wales (formerly Llyn Tegid Foel, named for Her consort, Tegid), fits the bill quite nicely.

Through the Gate of the Sea

Make sure you are sitting comfortably, with your eyes closed, and relax your body. Start with your left leg, tighten the muscles and then relax them. Then the right leg — tighten the muscles there, relax them, and let them go completely. Then your abdomen and stomach tighten the muscles up and then release them, let them go completely.

Now your chest and breathing muscles tighten them up and then relax them. Your back, shoulder, and neck muscles, tighten them up as tight as they'll go and as you release them feel the tension of the day just draining away. It's a wonderful feeling. Now your head and face muscles tighten them up as tight as they'll go. Tighten them up as tight as they'll go and then relax them. Lastly, do the muscles of your arms. Tighten them up as tight as they'll go and then relax them, from the shoulders down to the finger tips.

Now become aware of the black nothingness around you. Feel yourself floating, and then moving forward, lifting, drifting away. As you feel yourself floating away, the blackness fades to grey, becoming like a foggy mist as you begin to descend.

Your feet make contact with a surface, and you find yourself sitting in a small round boat — a coracle — which is floating through the mist on a river. It gently moves towards a bank, and comes to a halt, and you climb out and onto the riverbank.

The riverbank is forested, but where you climbed out of the coracle there is a pathway leading into the forest, and you follow it. The path is narrow, and twists and turns through the trees as it takes you deep into the heart of the forest until you find yourself at the door of a small cottage in a clearing.

The door opens before you can knock, and you enter, noting the large hearth, with a great cauldron set over it, steaming gently. Sitting in a chair beside the hearth is an old lady, wrapped in a shawl, tending to her hearth. Although you get the impression of great age, she is most certainly not frail or helpless, for this is Cerridwen, tending her mighty cauldron…

(pause for conversation with Cerridwen)

The time comes for you to continue along the path, and so you take your leave of her, and return to the forest outside.

You set off on the path that leads on from the clearing, a wider, straighter path that keeps the sky visible above. Before you know it, you find yourself approaching a quayside, down by the river. A coracle much larger than yours is docked there, upon which sits a majestic figure, surrounded by a pack of hounds. You step on board, and introduce yourself to Gwynn ap Nudd…

(pause for conversation with Gwynn ap Nudd)

This time your coracle is moored right next to Gwynn ap Nudd's larger one. Carefully, you climb into it once more, and no sooner are you seated than it begins to move away from the bank, taking you into the mist, which gets thicker and thicker, until all you can see is the coracle. Soon the mist closes in completely, leaving you in a featureless grey expanse as you feel yourself floating up and back.

The grey mist fades to black, and you feel yourself returning to the place you started from, sitting with your eyes closed. Sit up and open your eyes. The journey is over.

North

The Northern Airt is the Gate of Sky. This is the velvet darkness of midnight, where the Mother of Winds calls to Her Children.

The deities who guard this gate are Sky Gods, or associated with heights and winds. Arianrhod, Lady of the Silver Wheel, has strong stellar associations, as does Nuit, the Egyptian deity whose name is synonymous with night.

Male sky deities are rarer, but where there is sky there is weather, and most pantheons have an Old Thunderer who can lend His services to guarding this gate. Taran or Taranis is an old British Thunder God, and for the more Northerly inclined Thor makes an excellent choice. However, my Path departs from the obvious here, and works with Nectan, Keeper of the Sacred Well of Initiation used in the rite of Accolade for each of the Knights of the Table Round. This may seem counter-intuitive, and is certainly not easy to explain in writing, but sometimes the focus is not on that which casts the lightning bolt, but on that which calls the lightning strike to it.

Through the Gate of the Sky

Make sure you are sitting comfortably, with your eyes closed, and relax your body. Start with your left leg, tighten the muscles and then relax them. Then the right leg — tighten the muscles there, relax them, and let them go completely. Then your abdomen and stomach tighten the muscles up and then release them, let them go completely.

Now your chest and breathing muscles tighten them up and then relax them. Your back, shoulder, and neck muscles, tighten them up as tight as they'll go and as you release them feel the tension of the day just draining away. It's a wonderful feeling. Now your head and face muscles tighten them up as tight as they'll go. Tighten them up as tight as they'll go and then relax them. Lastly, do the muscles of your arms. Tighten them up as tight as they'll go and then relax them, from the shoulders down to the finger tips.

Now become aware of the black nothingness around you. Feel yourself floating, and then moving forward, lifting, drifting away. As you feel yourself floating away, the blackness fades to grey, becoming like a foggy mist as you begin to descend.

Your feet make contact with a surface, and you find yourself sitting in a small round boat — a coracle — which is floating through the mist on a river. It gently moves towards a bank, and comes to a halt, and you climb out and onto the riverbank.

The riverbank is forested, but where you climbed out of the coracle there is a pathway leading into the forest, and you follow it. The path is narrow, and twists and turns through the trees as it takes you deep into the heart of the forest, where you find a most pleasant glade. The ground is dotted with foxgloves taking advantage of the dappled shade, and a rocky outcrop supports a waterfall that pours down through a giant hag-stone. Standing beside the waterfall is a man in simple hermit's robes, and you hear him introduce himself to you as Nectan, Keeper of the Well, as he gestures to a small brick-built well at the edge of the clearing…

(pause for conversation with Nectan)

Nectan points out that it is getting late, and bids you continue along your way. You make your farewells, and set off on the path that leads on from the clearing, a wider, straighter path that keeps the sky visible above. Before you know it, you find yourself approaching a tall tower as the dusk closes in around you.

The open doorway leads to a staircase spiralling up the inside the tower, to a platform high above the trees. On reaching the top, you notice that it is quite dark now, and that there is a lady of regal bearing standing there, waiting for you: Arianrhod waits to talk with you about the stars…

All too soon it is time to move on again, and descending the stairs, you head for the edge of the clearing, aware of her piercing gaze watching you from the tower's top.

This time the path leading away from the clearing curves sinuously this way and that, in great lazy loops, until before you know it, you find yourself at the riverbank again. Although this is much further downstream, the coracle has floated down this far and is waiting for you. Carefully, you climb into it once more, and no sooner are you seated than it begins to move away from the bank, taking you into the mist, which gets thicker and thicker, until all you can see is the coracle. Soon the mist closes in completely, leaving you in a featureless grey expanse as you feel yourself floating up and back.

The grey mist fades to black, and you feel yourself returning to the place you started from, sitting with your eyes closed. Sit up and open your eyes. The journey is over.

Cross-Quarters

One of the significant differences between Wicca and traditional Witchcraft is the use of Cross Quarters. Four more gates, which lead to realms that hold initiatory Lore and experiences. Some Traditions have these gates guarded by deities, some by magickal creatures, such as dragons, or the traditional mythical beasties such as dragon, unicorn, mermaid and Pegasus, or the lion, eagle, bull and human of St John. In Old Craft Traditions, the Cross Quarters tend to be more primal, and more powerful than the more anthropomorphical Quarter points. The Quarters tend to deal with the Lore of the Bright Gods, made in the image of humanity, while the Cross Quarters deal with the Titanic forces from the dawn of existence. As such, they tend to be introduced to the more advanced students who have a good grasp of the Quarter Lore.

North-East

The North-East is a traditional direction from which to enter sacred space, and it is also a place where powerful external forces are at play on the Compass. In the old stone circles of Britain, the North-East is the place where the heel-stone is often found, a single standing stone that sits alone outside the circle proper. It is usually attributed to the Dark Mother, or the Black Goddess, who is known by various names like Black Anna or Black Annis.

The guardian of this gateway is the Queen of Northgales, one of the four Queens who accompanied Arthur to Avalon. Named in Mallory's version of the tale as Annowre, a Medieval version of the name Anu, or Black Annis.

South-East

The South-East is the direction of the Greenwood, the primal forest of tall trees, lush undergrowth and mossy rock. It is pregnant with potential and throbbing with life.

The guardian of this gateway is Morgan le Fey, half-sister of Arthur and one of the four Grail Queens who accompanied him to Avalon.

South-West

The South-West is the home of the Mystical Island in the centre of the sacred lake. It is reached through heroic effort.

The guardian of this gateway is the Lady of the Lake, who is also one of the four Grail Queens.

North-West

The North-West is the realm of the Wasteland, a very special place that is the gateway to initiation.

The guardian of this gateway is the Queen of the Wasteland.

The Cycle of Ced and Celi

The Quarters and Cross-Quarters can be seen as two sets of overlapping quarters, as in the diagram above. This has several advantages over the more typical eight-spoked wheel, because it gives a strong sense of the overlap in roles of the various deities, as well as making use of the traditional symbol of the Celtic Rose, which has four petals instead of the more common five, and which was used in East Anglia as a symbol for the Cunning Arts — especially in the form of the knot pattern known as the Celtic Rose. But it can also be found from time to time in the form of the Tudor Rose, once again as a symbol of Witchcraft (also found — rarely — in a six-petal version, representing the Hex Star.). Plus, this way, the quarters and cross-quarters are truly "quarters" rather than "eighths".

The Quarter Deities are the familiar ones that are mentioned above, but the Cross-Quarter Deities have a special relationship.

Ced and Celi

According to Owen Morgan, the author of Light of Britannia, Ced is the primal Black Mother who exists before manifestation. She/Her womb is the Great Enclosure. Her consort is Celi, the Unmanifest Sun, All Father to her All Mother.

The Rose of Ced and Celi

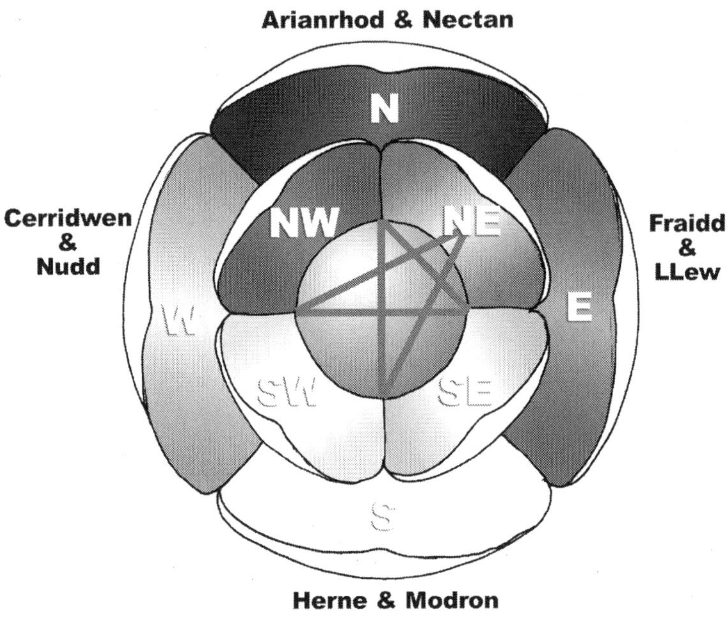

NE - Hu & Calen
SE - Alawn & Morwyn
SW - Plennydd and Blodwen
NW - Gwron and Tynghedwen

The Gods

Their son is Hu Gadarn, also known as Hesu the Mighty, who is born at the Winter Solstice, and follows the circuit of the Sun as Solar Deity until Spring Equinox. At this point, he becomes, through a state akin to puberty, Alawn (Father Hermes). At Midsummer he becomes Plenydd (Sun Longest Day), and at the Autumn Equinox, he becomes Gwron (Hero). These Latter three comprise the \|/.

Hu Gadarn

Hu the Mighty was the leader of the Cymry, and was reputed to have led them to Ynys Prodain (Britain) from Deffrobani (The Summer Realms). During a great flood, caused by the giant beaver Afanc, he enticed the beast from Itys Lake with the aid of a young girl, and while it slept with its head on her lap, he bound it with iron chains. The chains were attached to Hu's oxen, who were strong enough to drag the Afanc through the mountains, ploughing a pass through the mountains and imprisoning the Afanc in the lake LynnFfynnon Las.

Alawn, Plennydd and Gwron

The three primitive Bards, the disciples of Tydain Tad Awen by whom Druidism was founded. A Druidic movement being started would be presided over in turn by a Plenydd or light-bringer, a Gwron or stabilizer, and an Alawn or harmonizer, and so on in succession. According to Owen Morgan, the Earth is the Ox-Pen of the Bards, and these are the three great bulls which form the Triad of the Sun, or the Head of the Dragon.

The Goddesses

Hu's consort is Calen (the Earth), and she matches his transformations, becoming Morwyn (Holy Maid of Sea Foam), who is also Venus. At Midsummer she becomes Blodwen (Holy Flora), and at Autumn Equinox Tynghedwen (Holy Fortune) or Tynghedwen-Dyrraith (Fecundity/Barrenness). These latter three comprise /|\.

Calen

Calen is Mother Earth (a manifestation of Ced, the Enclosure).

Morwyn, Blodwen and Tynghedwen

According to Owen Morgan, these three are the three great cows which form the Triad of the Earth, or the Dragon's Tail.

Root and Crown
The Bilé Tree Turned Upside Down

Practically anywhere you look within the various indigenous religions of Europe, you will come across the World Tree, and in many religions of other lands too. Whether it is the World Ash, Yggdrasil, the Celtic Bilé Tree, the stang of the Anglo-Saxon Witch, or the Celestial Pole of various traditions, rumoured to originate in the magic and philosophy of Egypt — both Pharaonic and Coptic — the concept of a structure that both defines and bridges between the realms is powerful and nearly universal.

As a tool of cosmology, the Tree or Pole serves a useful function, and has been expanded in the Qabalah to become a veritable filing cabinet, route map and curriculum that is both elegant and complex. But for the practicing modern Cunning Folk, the Tree itself is a potent tool for working magic, in addition to its use in exploring the realms.

For many of us, the Bilé Tree is first and foremost the vertical axis of our Compass. At its root we find Annwn, the Underworld, home of the Cauldron of Rebirth. In the middle is Abred, the physical realm, and at its crown is Gwynvid, or Heaven. Of course, for Crafters there is often a twist to the general philosophy, and here we find the twist to be almost literal, as the Cunning Folk like their World trees to be topsy-turvy, and invert the Tree so that the Underworld is above, and Heaven is below. The reason for this is that the apparent paradox reveals a Mystery, which is often referred to as the stars reflected in the water. Simply put, we are the stars reflected in the water, and this manifests on many levels. Aleister Crowley was fond of the quote from his "Book of the Law" that states "every man and woman is a star", and this is another way of expressing the Mystery that manifests in the mundane world as the fact that the carbon that is part of the molecular structure of every living thing on earth originates in the stars and the sun, carried here across time and space. So we are literally made of the stuff of stars.

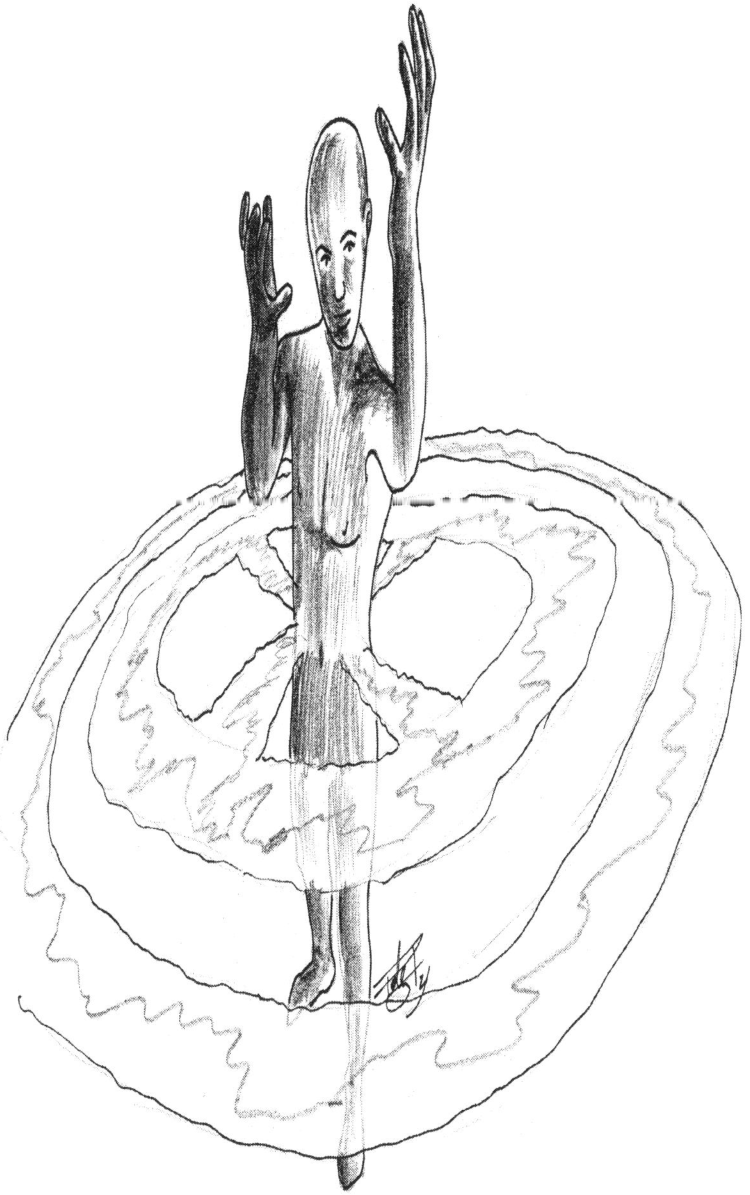

The Walking Crooked Path

Sacred Space

Sacred space means different things to different people. So really, the only way I can get around that is to tell you what it means to me. Sacred space is an enclosure we create, if you like, an artificial bubble in mundane reality, inside which we create an environment that is conducive to whatever type of ritual work or crafting work we plan on doing.

Now there are a lot of different methods in different traditions on creating sacred space. A lot of different names too. For the average Neopagan Wiccan, circle casting is the term that springs to mind. But circle casting is not exactly what the traditional Witch or cunning folk or traditional crafter would call the setting up of their sacred space. The reason for this is down to good old fashion history, and the fact that Crafters are not likely to use terms that have been borrowed from other places.

You see, circle casting is technically a ceremonial magic technique, and as Wicca borrowed quite a lot of its ritual structure from ceremonial magic, from the Golden Dawn, courtesy of Gerald Gardener and even more so Alex Sanders, who got even more ceremonial than Gerald did. So the circle casting that you have in most Wiccan covens is very ceremonial oriented. It uses the classical elements or the Watch Towers as they're often called. Even the phrase that is used when drawing the circle, in Gardnerian and Alexandrian circles at least, is taken straight out of the Key of Solomon:

> *"I conjure thee, o circle of power, that thou be'est a boundary between the world of men and the realms of the mighty ones; a guardian and protection that shall preserve and contain the power that I shall raise within thee. Wherefore do I bless thee in the names of the Lord and Lady."*

Or words to that effect.

So, it's very much about creating a barrier, a boundary within which you can work. And perhaps the most significant difference from the point of view of a crafter between the ceremonial or Wiccan circle and the sacred space created by non-Wiccan methods is that in a Wiccan circle, in a ceremonial circle, the aim is to set up an environment. And then bring everything you need into that environment. So you call upon your deities and bring them into the circle with you, drawing down the Moon, drawing down the Sun, invoking, bringing things in. This is very much the modus operandi of the ceremonial magician. He stays put and everything comes to him or her.

In traditional crafting, it actually works the other way around. The space is warded, or set aside if you like. And then the crafter takes the space and themselves to where ever it is the entities or energies that they want to work with happen to be. So, there's a definite difference in feel, if nothing else. There's also a difference in names.

Most traditional crafters try to avoid saying "casting circle" unless they really have to, just because they want to emphasize the fact that it's different from what a Wiccan does. Names that you might find being used for creating sacred space, warding the space, laying a compass, ploughing the bloody acre, raising the hedgerow, lots of different terms like that, which tend to be very physical-sounding descriptive terms. And each of them has a particular technique associated with it.

Some are use predominantly by a particular tradition, and some are more generic. Warding the space is probably the most generic term. It covers all the techniques for doing this. And it just involves essentially — and there are traditional crafters that are going to hate me saying this — casting a circle by another name. It is making the space in which you're standing something special, set aside from the mundane world.

Laying a Compass is a little bit more technical than just warding space, because what you're aiming to do is to set out the lie of the land, which is a very old fashioned sort of phrase, but it involves basically setting out things that are specific to your tradition and establishing their relationship to each other within the space and placing yourself in the centre or fulcrum-point, so that you're able to bring about the changes that you want.

And it takes a little bit of practice. Laying the Compass is not something you can learn from a book. It's something you really have to either get a light bulb moment about, or have somebody who is skilled at it work you through it. Like most traditional crafting techniques, it's all very experiential. You have to actually learn it hands on. So I'm not going to try to explain it in detail here, except basically what you're trying to do is you're trying to superimpose your tradition's map of the universe upon the land upon which you're working.

Ploughing the bloody acre is more of an outdoor term. It often involves the traditional image of dragging your left leg or your right leg, usually left leg, as you work your way around the perimeter of the circle space to establish a boundary marker, if you like. And the bloody acre is the area that is covered by the river of blood. It's a nice technical term, as used in fairy faith as well as several other old crafting traditions, that it's basically the current of magic or crafting that the practitioner is part of, so you're talking about immersing yourself in the current, in the tradition itself.

"Ploughing" is working the land quite literally, and making the two one and the same, because all traditions, all currents come out of the land in one form or another, because they're tied into the Ancestors which we'll be talking about later.

So do we do this indoors or outdoors? Well, as I was taught, if you can't work your magic stark naked in a concrete bunker, then you can't work magic period. So ultimately it doesn't matter. But obviously sometimes you're going to be working indoors and sometimes you're going to be working outdoors. Does the technique change? Yes it does, mainly because traditional crafters tend to see all of the land outdoors as sacred to a greater or lesser extent. So you don't really need to make the land sacred — it is already.

So when working outdoors, you just basically set up your boundary markers and you do your work, and usually at the end of it, rather than taking it all down again, you just walk away from it, because you're not going to de-sanctify the land, any more than you're going to make it more sacred than it started out to be.

Indoors is a different matter. If you work in a temple, then you're going to build up a similar sort of effect over the years in your temple space as well. But if you have to use the living room or a corner of your bedroom, then you're basically going to put it up and take it down each time as completely as you can so that you don't have any issues with using that space for mundane purposes at other times

Laying the Compass

For many practitioners of Traditional Witchcraft, the act of preparing the Sacred Space for ritual is known as Laying the Compass. Superficially, it resembles the Wiccan practice of casting circle, but it is done in quite a different way, and for quite different reasons.

Before we get into the practicality of this, I think it is important to take a look at the Compass itself, what it is and how we can use it. Probably one of the most important tools for the practitioner, the Compass exists as a concept, a "map" as a working tool (of the non-physical variety) and as a training aid.

As a training aid, we have already encountered the Compass — in many ways, those diagrams of the Wheel of the year are very much this aspect of the Compass. In other words, it acts as a framework upon which we can "hang" our deities, energies, stories and so on, and examine the relationships between them in order to gain insights. I should stress that any such use — no matter how based in Lore, Tradition and ancient practice — is purely arbitrary. The Compass in this mode is a construct that we fashion for our own use, and it does not define ultimate reality on any level.

Think of it as a test pattern, that we use to try out the "fit" of things. Where something makes sense, we can use its position and relation to other things to help us understand Lore, to construct rituals and to generally expand our understanding of the universe. But if it does not make sense, we can try a different position, and work with it until we find a workable relationship. So in this way, the Compass can act as a template for ritual construction, or as a way to try out a theory before committing to an actual working.

Its role as a concept is equally fluid, though it changes much less frequently. We have all come across the term "moral compass", and this is a concept that fits well here, if we replace moral with ethical. It cannot be stressed strongly enough that the Crooked Path is a path that requires the practitioner to be ethical rather than moral.

Morals are rules laid out by a person or organization. The Christian Ten Commandments are a moral code, to be followed without exception. And that is a good thing, because they provide an framework of ethical behaviour that can be followed without too much thought. But a Witch or Cunning Man needs to take responsibility for their own actions. Blindly following a moral code is fine for a beginner, but it presupposed a universe of stark black and white, and the universe we live in is made of endless shades of grey. So instead of the moral code of "do not steal", the Witch follows the ethical route, where the theft is weighed for its position on a sliding scale. Theft is wrong, but allowing a child to starve is more wrong, so if your child is starving and there is no better way, stealing that loaf of bread becomes a lesser wrong. You might be arrested and placed in a cell for the theft, but that is a small price to pay for the continued life of your child.

That phrase, the "price to pay" is the key here. For Cunningfolk, the real question becomes, "am I willing to pay the price for what I do?" This is why the Crooked Path is unlike Wicca with is "harm none" moral code. Sometimes it is okay to harm others, whether it is taking the life of an animal in order to feed, or taking the life of someone who threatens the life of your loved ones, or yourself.

So we cannot stress enough that by taking upon yourself the act of laying a Compass, you are placing yourself at the centre, the fulcrum or balance-point, where you are responsible for the things that are done within that sacred space.

The practical technique of laying the Compass is known by several other names: ploughing the bloody furrow, raising the grove, raising the hedgerow, calling the Land, calling the Moat, and other such names. There are countless variations of the physical process, but here is a description of the most common — at least, in my experience.One or two people enter the space, and begin circling about the centre. If it is two people, they sort of half face each other, and try to keep the centre between them, so they are forming the ends of the diameter of the Compass space. This often involves a sort of semi-crouching sideways walk, and it usually starts slow and gets faster as the intensity builds. A solo Compass layer will do much the same, but might drag their trailing leg as if literally ploughing a furrow in the ground with it. As the intensity builds, they may start rhythmically clapping or slapping their legs, as breathing becomes laboured and grunts and other sounds escape them. Finally, if there is a pair, they grasp hands or embrace in the centre, and the Compass is laid.

Not surprisingly, it is the non-physical part of the exercise that is most important. As the person or persons circle about, they see themselves digging deeper into the ground, as if digging a ditch or trench with their feet, and this usually continues until they feel themselves about knee-deep in the Land. At this point, the idea is to build up some resistance to their movement, as if they were pushing a boulder around the trench. Usually the boulder is not visualized, but rather the person or pair "feel" the effort and push against it. This psychic "friction" builds the energy and the tension to a point where the space within the trench or moat becomes "separate" from mundane reality, which is perceived as a thickness in the air and a sense of timelessness. Coming to a stop frequently invokes dizziness in the participants, even though the circling motion itself does not make them dizzy.

Next, everyone involved in the working needs to enter the Compass, and this is done by either the person who laid the Compass or the Guardian laying a broom across the entry way so that the bristles are outside and the end of the handle is inside the moat. At this point the sacred space is perceived as if it were a boat moored at the quay-side, and each person enters by tapping their left foot on the broom and turning widdershins into the space, as if they were climbing over an old stile to get over the fence or hedge between two fields.

When there is a group, such as a full coven, working together, there are a few considerations to be noted. Firstly, the person officiating or facilitating the work needs to claim the space and take the Compass for their own, and the other participants need to acknowledge this and surrender the Compass to the leader — an act of great trust. This is facilitated by the use of a coin to "pay for the Land". By paying the coin, the leader becomes — temporarily — sovereign over the Land, and is able to take possession of it fully. In coven structures, this is often done by the Magister giving a coin to the Guardian, who taps it three times on the broom before stepping over it, and then presenting the coin to the Ancestors on the Magister's behalf, before depositing it on or near the hearthstone. Obviously for solo or small informal workings, the leader can do this themselves, but in a coven, this esoteric equivalent of "power of attorney" gives the Guardian the authority to override the Magister for reasons of safety, and so on.

Treading The Mill

Unlike raising the Cone of Power, this practice is less about raising energy, and more about creating a vortex. Also known as the Widdershins Walk, this is the way to descend to the Wasteland, where we can work directly with our most ancient Ancestors. Craftings involving treading the Mill are generally concerned with moving between the Worlds or opening a portal between the worlds in order to affect an exchange of some sort. An excellent example is what we do at Samhain, when we open a gateway into the Mound to allow the spirits of the recently departed — gathered by the Wild Hunt — to be escorted into the Land of the Dead where they will be placed in the Cauldron of Cerridwen for rebirth.

This is not a technique that anyone would call fun, except that we all seem to be addicted to doing it… it has some superficial resemblances to laying the Compass, except that it is always widdershins (well, there

is a deosil version, but used for very specific reasons), and there is no attempt to focus on an outcome or a "result". In fact, it is important for the participants to surrender to the brutality of the physical process, leaving just the Mill leader to guide and control it.

Physically, there are two ways of doing the Mill that I have learnt — I'm sure there are others too. The first of these is the way that the Clan of Tubal Cain does it. They place a focal point, such as a candle, at the centre, and extending their left arms, point at the flame with their index finger. Turning their head to the left, they sort of cock it backwards, so that their left cheek is over their left shoulder and they are able to sight down the length of their arm and finger. This is described obliquely in the Cochrane letters, alluding to the way a cow looks over her shoulder, and it results in both a visual effect (from gazing at the candle flame surrounded by swirling circular movement) and a slight restriction of blood-flow to the brain, which combine to create a powerful trance state. This technique is most effective for oracular work, or for seeking answers and guidance.

The other method, which we use in Briar Rose, is mostly used for taking the entire coven to the wasteland or some other realm, where they interact with entities or do a crafting together. It opens doorways in a very physical, visceral way, such as when it is done to open the Mound at Samhain.The technique this time is to tramp around the circle widdershins, with your eyes loosely focused on the back of the person in front of you. The centre of gravity is lowered by bending the knees and curving the back so that everyone is in a crouching gait, and each step includes swaying to the side where the foot is planted, giving everyone a shuffling, side to side gait, so we almost zigzag around the circular path. Like the Compass, the goal is to get the feeling you are pushing against an obstacle and sinking into the ground. A slow chant is used to keep everyone in step like a chain gang, because it is important that nobody has a single thought about the goal or purpose of the task at hand, but rather they all mindlessly stumble along behind the one in front, as if they are joined by a chain to the leader. The Mill does not speed up — if anything, it is likely to slow a little — but it gets more and more intense, until the participants are feeling real discomfort, bordering on agony as the pressure build. When the leader feels the whole thing is ready to burst, they yell "down!", and everyone drops to the ground and releases the pent-up tension and energy, which is directed by the leader to open the portal, push unwanted things into the void, or upon up the vista of the realm being visited.

The Cone

Raising the Cone of Power is a technique that can be found in the Gardnerian Book of Shadows, Katherine Kurtz's Lammas Night, and most forms of Traditional Witchcraft. The details may vary, but the overall effect is the same. This is the technique that the Witches of England were said to have used to defend Britain from the Nazis during World War II.

The technique that we use is for everyone to stand in a circle. The person or thing the energy is being raised for is placed in the centre if possible, or if not a photo, some other representation, or just visualization will suffice.

The leader of the cone starts everyone swaying from side to side, beginning a chant such as:

"Circle, circle, power build
Open, open, be ye filled."

When the momentum is built up enough, the leader begins to step deosil around the circle, and the others follow suit. It is helpful to have a few experienced crafters spread evenly about the circle. The circling begins painfully slowly, and gradually builds up to a run. Experienced crafters can try the classic Witch-step, where you step to the left with your right foot, crossing in front of the left foot, as you look left, then step to the left again with the left foot. The next step with the right foot goes behind instead of in front of the left foot, turning the face to the right. It is difficult to describe, but when competently performed it is graceful and filled with power.

Although the momentum builds steadily until everyone is running around the circle, the leader "pulls back" as much as possible, making the chanting lag behind the steps just enough to apply the brakes. This is to create tension, friction, and maximize the amount of energy generated. As soon as the leader feels the energy reach its peak, they yell for everyone to stop and direct the energy at the target.

Part of the trick for the rest of the group is to follow the leader and maintain a balance point in the work, while not focusing too much on the details. I find that I usually end up reaching a point where I begin to see a blue dragon racing around the working deosil, while a red one races widdershins. To be in the centre of such a working as the energy is released is to be awed, inspired.

Libation

For a Wiccan, this is "cakes and ale" and is a sharing of food and drink that has a great deal of symbolism and meaning attached to it. For the Traditional Crafter, this goes deeper still. Known most often by its Cornish name of "Houzle", the coming together of white bread and red wine or dark ale is seen as honouring the blood and bone of the Ancestors. This is a complex piece of symbolism, considering how simple the practical technique itself it. The libator dips the bread in the wine or ale, and toasts the Ancestors, the Gods, old Hornie, and whoever else they need to honour. In a group, the participants take turns. It seems very simple, but the symbolism runs very deep, as in addition to the act of symbolic theophagy that can be seen in the Catholic Mass, there is also the nature of blood and bone to take into account. Frequently the blood is seen as the lineage itself — the Witch-Blood — and the bone is the body of Lore that both sustains the blood and enables us to discover and connect with it.

Traditionally, the Houzle is performed with a horn cup, which — depending on the tradition — can be an actual cup made of horn or a stirrup cup (the cup designed originally for members of the fox hunt to drink their libation before the hunt. They do not have a base, but rather are stored upside down, and are frequently made in the shape of animals, especially stags and foxes.)

Riding the Dragon

Many Traditional Crafters have an interesting relationship with dragons. Some see them as archetypes, some as being similar to the Gods, and some see them as living mythical beasts, in a very literal way. It is certainly true that myths and legends involving dragons are central to many of the traditional cultures from which British Witchcraft derives. In Sumerian and Babylonian mythology we have Tiamet, the Mother of Dragons, and even in the Ancient Egyptian Mysteries we can find the dragon tucked away — take a good look at the figure of Ptah found in the tomb of Tutankhamun, and you will see the markings of feathered wings wrapped around His mummiform body. Ptah, the Great Architect, and one of the oldest gods in the Egyptian pantheon, is a dragon.

But for us in Briar Rose, the dragon is a very personal thing, because we see drakes to a certain extent as "all of the above", but most importantly, we see the drake as part of our own make-up. Just as Orion Foxwood teaches that we have three selves, the Dream Walker, Surface Walker and Star Walker, so in our kind of crafting we work with three aspects of self, the Drake, the Initiate and the Crown. In other Traditions these also appear, though they may have different names, such as the Fetch-Beast, the Magician and the Star-Body, or Shadow-Self, Self and Star-Self.

For us, the Drake is the Underworld component of our being, the Shadow form from which we gain our power. So awakening the Dragon is an important part of our development, and a key part of our rite of initiation. However, there is a caveat, because the Drake needs to be reined in by the Crown or Higher Self, otherwise it is out of control, and will ride roughshod over the Initiate self. It is much like the relationship between Set and Nephthys in the Egyptian Mysteries — Set is, among other things, the chaotic yet potent power of the desert storm, wild and destructive. But Nephthys provides the control and contact for his chaos, giving form to his force so that the power is tamed and becomes her power of dissolution, the side of nature that involves breaking down things to their basic building blocks through erosion, decay and rotting, so that those components can be recycled and incorporated in new growth, new life.

So the key when working with drakes is to find the balance point, much like finding the fulcrum point of the Compass in order to work magic... only the Drake is the engine that powers the magic, and the Compass is the tool we use, guided by our Higher Self or Crown, to direct it. We use the term "riding the dragon" both for the process of balancing this relationship, and also for the exercise we use to learn and practice it.

> The exercise of riding the dragon is similar in some aspects to a martial arts exercise, as it involves directing energy through posture. Start by standing with your feet shoulder-width apart. Bend your knees to lower your centre

of gravity, and curve your spine, so it is a little like sitting in an imaginary chair or saddle. You should lift your heels off the ground slightly, and allow your ankles and knees to flex slightly. This results in a gentle bobbing motion, which should be matched to your breathing. Try to curve your back a little more, so the upper part is also curved. Let your head drop forward and down, and then look up, curving the neck. Finally, hold your arms and hands out before you, though they should be curved as well, as if you are holding a large invisible beach ball in front of you. This is the basic rider position.

Now reach down with your senses, feeling for the dark pulsing energy that "bobs" in time to your own motion. This is your Drake. Draw it up until you feel almost as if your feet will leave the floor, and be aware of the Drake flexing in time with you between your thighs. At this point things will start to get warm, and you will feel spontaneous movements ripple through your spine and neck. This is where you need to find the balance point, which allows the energy to move where you want it, without it getting away from you. It is a bit like riding a unicycle. As long as there is balance, you will find that gentler controlled movement is easy and flows well, and the whole thing feels like an extension of yourself — but lose that point of balance and it will quickly get away from you, and suddenly you are being forced to move, dragged in the direction it wants to go, because you have lost control.

I won't beat about the bush — this is a dangerous exercise, and should be practiced at first only for a short time, five or ten minutes, preferably with someone to keep an eye on you. Because the ramifications of letting your Drake get control of you, instead of vice-versa, is that it won't just take you for a ride (and a tempting, rollercoaster ride it will be), but it will take control of your thought, emotions and every aspect of your life too, and this is not a good place to be. You won't even notice it yourself, but you would become a predator, drawing on the life-force of those around you, like a psychic vampire, taking risks both physical and spiritual, and eventually the unbalanced energy would consume you, but not before it wreaked havoc on the lives of those you care about. Once someone becomes dragon-ridden, the only way to deal with them is for someone experienced to shut them down, to make sure they have no further access to their dragon in this lifetime, which effectively ends their journey on the Path for this incarnation.

Awakening the Altar

Traditionally, crafters do not use altars in the same way that Wiccans or other religions do. For many spiritual paths, an altar is a combination of shrine and focal point of their worship. But traditional Crafters do not worship the Gods, and if they use an altar table at all, it is more akin to the ceremonial magician's use of the altar as a workbench. But we do pay our respects to our ancestors, and while the altar itself is just a table (in our case a very nice hand-carved and purpose-built one), it is the resting place for the tools we use to interact with our ancestors, the Hearth Stone, the Skull, the wand and the cup. So when we talk about awakening or activating the altar, we are really talking about opening up the gateway for the Ancestors.

This is one of those exercises that are very simple, and will almost seem silly until the first time you do it right. We have a bunch of candles on the altar, because we like to work in candle-light, but there are a set of candles around the skull and stone that are specifically there for the awakening process. We start by lighting these candles — a black one to the left of the skull, a white one to the right, a blue one behind the skull, and a red one upon its crown.

The black and white candles represent the pillars that mark the gateway, and the arrows that are often found attached to the stang, among other things. The blue and red candles represent in turn Noctifer and Lucifer, the two aspects of Venus, the Evening and Morning Star.

In many ways Noctifer and Lucifer are to the Tradition what the Dragon and Crown are to us as individuals. Noctifer is the dark twin, potent, passionate, chaotic and illogical, while Lucifer is the calm, intellectual and controlled one. They are, of course, both separate and the same, and can be found in such cultural pairings as Lugh and Cromh, Llew and Gronw, Osiris and Set.

Each of us has our own way of lighting the candles. Some use a few words, other do it in silence. The important thing is to acknowledge and feel the presence of the pillars and twins, and to be aware of their balance. Then we call in the Ancestors, by calling on our primary ancestor:

"Old XXX, bring them in,
Old XXX, bring them in,
Old XXX XXXXXX, bring them in,
One by one, and all together
Ancestors long gone, and those yet to be
Bring them in to dance ,
the dance of life and death with me."

Obviously the name of our primary ancestor is particular to us, and private, so I have replaced it with the XX's above.

Three times the wand is banged on the altar, then the crafter places his hands either side of the skull, and using bellows breathing (where the sacred space acts like a bellows, and it feels like the air is pushed and pulled from the crafter's lungs rather than simple inhale-exhale), the y start to build up energy in the breath, with every inhale going "right down to the boots", getting bigger with each breath, until by the third inhale the crafter draws breath in until their whole body is filled with energized air to the point where they can't hold it in any more. Then, the crafter exhales the charged air — life-force — into the mouth of the skull, as if giving mouth-to mouth resuscitation, breathing life into the skull. It is difficult to describe the process, but you will know when you get it right, because the skull will suddenly feel "enfleshed" in your hands, and with breathe back.

The ancestors are then welcomed, and a bell is rung to signal that we have moved between the worlds and are now in the presence of the Ancestors.

The Fetch

As if there weren't enough twists and turns in the Way of the Crafter already, there are at least three distinct things that can be referred to as a Fetch in modern crafting; the Fetch Beast, "fetch-and-carry", and the "shape-shifter's skin".

The Fetch-Beast, also known as the Fetch-Wife, has been dealt with elsewhere in this book, and is the Underworld Self of the Crafter, known in Briar Rose as the Dragon.

The third kind of Fetch, the one used in shape-shifting, is traditionally a piece of skin or fur belonging to the animal into which the Shape-shifter transforms. In some cases, such as the selkies in Ireland, it is the actual whole skin that the shape-shifter puts on to become the animal.

But when Witches refer to a Fetch, they usually mean the "thought-form" created for a specific purpose, to find something or someone, to bring people together, or carry out some other task. Ceremonial Magick has a similar technique, the main difference being the status of the Fetch… in the Craft, it is a living entity, whereas CMs tend to see them as servitors, something akin to astral droids.

To create a fetch, you need to start by pulling energy together in a concentrated form. There are many ways of doing this, but for a solo practitioner the most effective way is to visualize a ball of light between your hands, and pump energy into it from your core, through your hands. Keep pumping energy into it until it is really full, and you can feel the energy really strongly. Then you begin to shape it. You should have chosen an appropriate form before-hand — most Witches work with animal forms, and it is recommended to avoid using human forms unless you know what you are doing.

Once the fetch has its form, you should name it, bind it to its task, and then set its destruction fate. It is considered bad form to let a fetch exist longer than a year, so traditionally a cut off date is built in, so the fetch ceases to be on a certain date, or when the task is complete, whichever comes first. A fetch that is allowed to exist for too long, especially after their task is complete, can develop independence and start drawing off the life-force of its creator. State firmly the fetch's purpose, its cut off date, and name it, binding all these things together. Then release it to complete its task.

Raising the Flame

Raising the Flame is an interesting exercise, because it both embodies some key pieces of Lore that are common to many Traditions, and is a great example of Lore being directly "enfleshed" by a Tradition. Whether it is ancient Forge Fire or a simple candle flame, the idea of filling yourself with fire-energy is common to most traditions, but the Path of the Blacksmith can often be found hidden within the wider path of a particular Craft Tradition and it often manifests within that tradition as the Lore of Forge Fire.

Most cultures have a Blacksmith God, and the stories of Hephaestus, Vulcan and Weyland are well known, but less well-known is the Celtic equivalent, Goibhniu, who forged weapons and armour. But for the Welsh Crafter there is an even less well-known deity of the forge, and that is Fraidd (also spelt Ffraid), a Welsh aspect of Bridhe or Bridget — she is said to have sailed to Wales from Ireland on a sod of earth, which became a mound in the sea between Anglesey and Holy Isle.

There is a distinct connection between the forge-fire and the hearth-fire, or heart-fire, and this exercise makes good use of that.

> Raise the Compass, and place a candle in the East. You may embellish with a skull, hammer and tongs, etc, but the candle flame is the most important thing.
>
> Sitting down, enter a deep state, and visualize yourself expanding and contracting with each breath, like the bellows of a blacksmith.
>
> Take three deep breaths while blocking off the left nostril, and expand the visualization so that you are inside a giant bellows: when you breathe out it is the expanding of the bellows that is sucking the air out of you, and when you inhale, it is the contracting of the bellows that is pushing the air into you.
>
> Let the bellows-wind that is being blown into you fan the smouldering flame within you, making it brighter as it dances up your spine. Keep this up as the fire expands within your body. Feel the sexual heat of arousal – a side-effect of the fanning of the flame.
>
> You will get to a point where you feel very warm and empowered, but don't stop there. With intent and focus, take a deep slow breath and use it to push the flame down deep into the earth beneath you, down to the forge of the Old One at the heart of the Earth. When you exhale, draw that fire back up into your body, rising up your spine through your loins, belly and heart to your head. Let it really infuse your spine and head.

This fire that returns is not just the Fire you sent down. It contains the Fiery Blood of the Land, of the Underworld, the Transforming Fire of the Forge God Himself. Let your arms raise as the Fire rises, then exhaling again, let the Flame return partially to the ground, to complete the circuit, and bind you to the Land.

Sit and contemplate the Old One, relaxed and breathing normally.

The more you do this, the more it will affect you.

A Crooked Sixpence

There are plenty of spells from various traditions that use coins, especially silver coins. Even in Hoodoo and Conjure - which are uniquely American traditions borne of the union of European and African folk magic, with a healthy dose of Native American lore for seasoning - you will find that the "Mercury Dime" is favoured. This is a ten-cent coin that depicts the winged head of Liberty, but it is easy to see why it was mistaken for the Roman God Mercury. It was minted between 1916 and 1945, and is used as a good luck charm or for prosperity, especially by gamblers. Mercury dimes minted in a Leap Year are said to carry double the luck.

For those of a British persuasion, the coin of choice is the silver sixpence, once ubiquitous as the token placed in every Christmas pudding, to give luck to the one who found it — providing they didn't swallow it, of course. There are many things about the sixpence that makes it particularly valuable to the crafter, especially in modern times.

Firstly, as a coin, it has been around for a very long time. The first sixpence was struck for Edward VI in 1551, and it was legal tender until decimalization in 1971. It was also the last coin to be made of silver — until 1920 the sixpence was sterling silver, and in that year it was reduced to 50% silver. It was not until 1946 that the Treasury switched to cupro-nickel. So a pre-1946 coin has both the weight of history and real silver in its make-up. This made it especially valuable for spellcrafting, but the final clincher is its value, six pence for the six arms of the Hex Star.

Modern crafters have the additional advantage that it has been withdrawn from circulation. It is no longer legal tender in this realm, making it "legal tender" in the next world instead. The old custom was to bend a coin, rendering it useless for mundane purposes, but now all sixpences come ready to use in the realms beyond this one.

Casting a Coin in the Well

If there is one spell that we like to use above all others in Briar Rose, it is this one. It is an old crafting that was used throughout Britain, though it is best documented in the Silver Bough, a wonderful collection of folklore and practices from Scotland.

Traditionally, this was performed at a well that was sacred to a local saint. The idea was to take your coin and a rag or length of rope, and, during the hours of darkness — ideally just before dawn — walk three times around the well, each time petitioning the saint for the desired outcome, and then throwing the coin into the well, after spitting on it or kissing it. The rag or rope was then tied upon the tree that was always associated with sacred wells, and head off away from the well, never looking back. The idea was to be out of sight of the well before sunrise.

Naturally, for most of us — especially those in the US — it is not easy to find an appropriate well that can be used for this. But in Briar Rose we have the good fortune to work with St. Nectan, the saint whose well was visited by the Knights of the Round Table before setting out on the quest for the Grail. Consequently we use the cauldron as a well for various workings, including skrying, and it lends itself nicely to this crafting.

First of all, we have a collection of silver sixpences that we use and reuse exclusively for crafting purposes. Prior to a working, each participant purchases a sixpence in exchange for a modern coin. We then open up our sacred space, place the cauldron (about half full of water) in the centre, and open the Well of the Ancestors. We do this by calling upon Nectan, and then we open the well in the cauldron using a technique very similar to the one Orion Foxwood uses to open the Faery Well.

> Start by feeling for the surface of the well. In our case, it is going to be the opening of the cauldron, so we pass our hands deosil around the lip of the cauldron, not quite touching it, feeling for the point of pressure where the worlds

meet. Once we feel that, we begin to open it up by dipping our fingers through the pressure "bubble" and creating an aperture that is widened to match the lip of the cauldron.

Once the well is opened, we call to the Ancestors, breathing life-force into our hands and offering it into the well, where we feel the Ancestors receiving it, and returning their own offering of life-breath into our hands. We take that up and inhale it. This is done three times, and then the Well is fully open.

Next, we all walk around the well three times, or more if we feel the need to "wind up the power", chanting or muttering as we go something appropriate to the working. Then each person in turn kisses or spits on the coin, depending on what is appropriate to the crafting being worked, and then throws the coin in the well. We then tie our rag or string to the Stang, representing the World Tree, and leave.

Later, after the evening's work is complete, we retrieve the coins and clean them for later use. The modern coins — legal tender — that everyone used to buy the sixpences are taken to a charity collection pot, or are left at a crossroads, depending once again on which is felt most appropriate for the working.

Another thing we do with the coins is that everyone has a sixpence that they keep in their left pocket. Whenever something is going on that they need to influence the outcome of, they reach into their pocket and turn the sixpence three times without removing it from the pocket. This is an old crafting tool, and I have developed the habit of giving a sixpence to anyone who visits our home, so they can keep it in their pocket for the same purpose. All the coins we use are early 20th century coins, though I did buy a beautiful specimen — well-worn and handled — from the reign of Queen Elizabeth I for my wife.

The Path of the Outcast

One of the aspects of walking the Crooked Path that is rarely addressed in books is the sense of being an outcast. What we're talking about is this sense of being isolated, of being alone even when you're in a crowd, even when within a crowd of Pagans, you'll sit apart from them. You feel like there's something between you and them that stops you from being a part of it. You feel very much alone. And it can be very disconcerting, especially when you're not sure where it's coming from.

So what causes this, because it seems to be a very universal experience that people have as they get deeper into a Pagan or magical path. And there are some very practical reasons for why this should occur. The first of these is that if you're following a magical path, you're going through experiences that can only be shared with others who have already been there before you, because nobody else would really understand. There are also experiences that you just don't have the words to explain, that even somebody else who's been there you can't really talk about either, because you can't find the words. You just have to hope that they've been there enough that they know what you're trying to say and get the gist of it that way. And then of course, if you have friends who aren't Pagan, if you talk to them about your experiences, they're going think you're a little flaky.

Even those who are Pagan friendly may not really understand what you're talking about, and may make light of it, or make you feel like uncomfortable in some way — without meaning to, of course. And this can get really, really depressing. I've known people who've had a terrible time, and this isn't something that goes away. I think I should warn you about this. I've been following this Pagan path for over twenty years now, and I still get it.

The thing is, even people who are Pagan don't always understand it, if they're not going into it as deeply as you are. You see, our path is tailored to us. We tailor it to suit our own needs, so even when we're in a coven or some other kind of group; it's still really just a bunch of individuals who happen to be traveling in the same direction for a while. It's a bit like caravanning or car pooling on a road trip. You didn't start out with these people. You may not end up with these people. But right now you all happen to be going to the same place at the same time. And so you travel together for convenience. But you're still very much an individual traveling along your own path.

There are also some magical reasons for this. Most people who practice a Pagan belief system, at the very least, work with meditation, altered states of consciousness. Those who follow a magical path can add to this practice such as walking between the worlds, astral travel, and other ways of actively exploring the realms. There's old term for people who do this sort of thing. They used to be called hedge-walkers or hedge-riders. Until fairly recently — the last hundred and fifty years or so ago — in the UK, movement from place to place was very restricted for common folk. Only the gentry, tinkers, and craftsmen could travel from place to place without permission from the lord of the manner. Craftsmen, of course, included healers, cunning folk and the like. In other words, people like us.

Magical folk, metaphorically and sometime literally, live on the outskirts of society. Most find it hard to relate to non-magical folk. Right from the beginning, that's how they end up getting into a Pagan or magical life style — because they finally found they could find people that they could relate to. And as they get deeper into their studies, they find this difficulty becomes much more pronounced. For example, as I said, I've been doing this Pagan magical stuff for over twenty years now, and I remember back in high school when I found it very difficult to understand why people didn't seem to be the way I was. I had a lot of trouble with people being selfish, petty and materialistic. I never really understood why. I mean, I had a generalized spirituality of my own, which other people didn't seem to bother with. And it was very, very confusing for me.

Finally, when I became a Pagan and started practicing, I found that there were other people, in fact, who had the same thoughts and feelings along those lines as I did, which made me feel a lot better. But even then, every now and then it would crop up that I felt that I was different or I was alone. There was a barrier between me and the rest of humanity and it got very disconcerting. This has happened, off and on, all the way through to the last couple of years when I really started to explore and understand what was going on for me, courtesy of the tradition that I now follow, where they actually recognized that this happens and start to teach you to deal with it.

You can't get rid of it but you can learn to handle it and the way you handle it is when you need to be alone, you go and be alone, and nobody bugs you for it. So that's really what it's all about. Even now, as I said, I'm following the tradition I've been searching for all of my life. I'm very, very lucky in that sense, yet even now, in the middle of a crowd of people who are all in my tradition, I can find myself going off and having some quiet time by myself, because I need to be apart, because I feel apart and alone. It's just one of those things. As I said, it doesn't go away. But knowing that other people are going through the same thing makes it a little easier to manage.

So, what are the benefits of this? I mean, if you've drawn the shitty card of being alone and on the edge of society as an outcast, why? What's the point of it all? There must be some benefit to it, otherwise people would have stopped doing it a long time ago, and there wouldn't be any Pagans or magical people anymore. Well, people drawn to this path usually have a voracious appetite for learning. On a purely practical level, it's easier to indulge this in solitude. As I said before, those of us who are part of a thriving Pagan community appreciate the gathering of like minded folk. But we will take ourselves away from time to time to work with the solitude. We can have too much even of our own type of people.

You see, those who are initiated into a tradition of any sort, be it Gardnerian Wicca, Alexandrian Wicca, any other sort of Wicca or Traditional Witchcraft or any other magical path, are twice born. They're set apart in the same way that the chosen people, the Hebrew consider themselves set apart by God. This automatically puts up a barrier between us and mundane folk. We're different, which is why we begin to mix only with those who are like us. Because it's easier to mix with people where there's less of a barrier. It's just human nature.

Besides, as we become more deeply involved, our beliefs, our values, and our ideas of good conduct change. Suddenly an evening swilling beer and watching sports just doesn't cut it anymore. I'm sure anybody who's been following this path for a little while has found that there are things that the people who they associate with out of habit do, that they just can't understand the point of anymore.

Unfortunately, this is a subject that's not often spoken about. So people experiencing it for the first time find themselves without a frame of reference. They don't know what the hell's going on, and it disturbs them. They decide that because they're feeling like an outsider, it's because they don't belong on the path, and then they leave it to find out what they do belong to. The trouble is, of course, that if you do belong on this path and walk away from it, you're still going to carry away the isolation and the sense of apartness with you. But on top of that you're going to add the stresses and trauma of not being true to yourself.

That's the main reason why I decided to talk about this subject today. In the hopes that those of you that are experiencing this side of the path, will recognize it for what it is, the calling to walk between worlds, to mediate as priesthood, to become the wise woman or cunning man. The knowledge of why you feel this way won't stop you feeling it. But you can draw ironic comfort that you are not alone in your isolation, that every true Witch feels it. It ebbs and flows. Sometimes you feel it more than other times. But remember, it is part of the mark of the witch. And it's the coin you pay in exchange for amazing experiences you have between the worlds. Yes, those same experiences that you just can't share with any but a select few.

Of Gods and Ancestors

Working with deities is an important part of any Tradition, though in Briar Rose, as in many other Craft Traditions, we do so less frequently than our neo-Pagan cousins. We tend to rely on our own abilities or those of our ancestors, coming to the Gods and Goddesses of our path primarily for rites of passage and initiation, or where a "hand greater than mine" is required. We also interact with the deities through exploring and experiencing their myths, bringing the Lore to life as a way of learning and growing spiritually.

There are several related techniques for working with deity, and while they might bear a superficial resemblance to certain Wiccan or even Christian practices, they are in fact quite different.

Contact

Invoking deity in Wicca ("drawing down the moon") and ceremonial magic involves opening yourself up and calling the deity to you, but for us the process is almost reversed. We journey between the world, where we call upon the deity or deities, and then rise up to meet them where they are. The interaction can be in the form of a contact or possession, the only real difference being the depth of trance-state involved and the degree of separation between deity and practitioner.

For a contact, the usual state is for the practitioner to be in the presence of the deity, and able to converse with them, but they maintain a distinct and separate identity. In a group working, the practitioner relays messages between the deity and those present in the rite, much like someone passing on the comments of someone on the phone to others present.

Possession

In possession, the separation between deity and practitioner is removed to a greater or lesser extent, allowing for a merging of the two. In this case, the practitioner "becomes" the deity, speaking as the deity and often taking on physical aspects of the deity.

In practice, the interaction between practitioner and deity fluctuates between mild contact and full possession, and it is experience that enables the person who has been practicing the Craft for a long time to maintain a strong possession. In any case, the possession usually lasts only as long as the deity concerned wishes.

The technique for controlling the contact or possession is remarkably simple — the practitioner, having used visualization to manipulate the trance-state and enter the realm of the deity, visualizes moving closer or further way from the deity to increase or decrease the level of "merging".

Patrons and Matrons

On the Path I follow, each of us works with a Patron and a Matron deity. Usually the first one to be encountered is the deity that shares the practitioner's gender, mostly because it always seems to be the first to arrive, and also the easiest to work with. Because we have found that possession by deity tends to be accompanied by temporary changes to posture and other manifestations of the nature of the deity, we tend to work cross-gender workings only after the practitioner's relationship with the "parent" of the same gender is well-established, so that they can mediate working with the opposite gender.

Contact/Possession Exercise

Set up ritual space in the usual way and, using the trance-inducing method you prefer, place yourself in a light trance state. Visualize yourself in a secluded place that is appropriate for the deity you are attempting to contact. Call out to them, and wait.

Soon, you will become aware of their presence, and you will see them standing a small distance away. Rise up and approach them slowly — you will "feel" the air thicken as you get closer, and there will come a point where you are close enough to converse in a quiet voice, and hear each other clearly. Usually there are three or four steps between you at this point. Stepping closer intensifies the experience, while stepping back reduces it. You find that at one-or two paces apart you feel yourself merging with the deity… the closer you are, the more "as one" you find yourself to be with the deity. Eventually, the deity will invite you to step in entirely, and you and they become one for a short time.

When you are ready to end the exercise, thank the deity and step back, away from them. Traditionally, three steps are taken backwards, facing the deity, before you turn and walk quietly away, yourself once more.

Working With Ancestors

So, who am I talking about when I refer to Ancestors? Obviously, the thing that springs to mind is grandma and grandpa and all of their kith and kin. But, hopefully we're going back a little further than that.

"Ancestors" is a word that gets thrown around a lot, and I don't know if everybody really sits and thinks about what they mean when they say it. We're obviously not just talking about grandparents, great grandparents and aunts and uncles when we're talking about ancestors. We're going back a little further than that, and referring to the pre-Christian ancestors who did the sort of things that we're hoping to reconstruct, recreate, and recover whatever phrase you want to use for it.

It really is meant to mean your blood ancestors, but in practice we're really talking about the ancestors of our race or our species. We tend to cast the net a little wider. We'll take anybody from way back when who has a nugget of lore or information that they want to share with us. So, we're really not that proud when it comes to stuff like that. We'll take it from anywhere. Ancestors are generally very important parts of traditional crafting. It's probably one of the biggest things that differentiates traditional craft from Wicca is the focus on ancestral workings. Gardnerian and Alexandrian Wicca does have ancestral workings, but they're not as well known or as obvious in most cases. But they do exist. But ancestral work within the Traditional Crafting community -if you can call it a community: a bunch of ornery individuals that I don't know if the word community applies here — but ancestors play a very important part in both the Wheel of the Year, rites of the year, and also the personal crafting of a Traditional Crafter.

So, it's important to get your bearings where the ancestors are concerned. Really, they are a very key component of most rituals and of the current of the Tradition in general. Obviously, they're seen in some mythic sense as being the progenitors of the tradition. And probably one of the most obvious signs of ancestral working in a coven or group will be some sort of stone and probably some sort of representation of a skull upon the altar at some point. On our altar we have a large hearth stone. And we have a pewter skull with Celtic markings sitting on top of that to represent our Ancestors.

I should point out at this point that the use of an altar itself is almost considered blasphemy in some traditional crafting circles. We happen to have a table that I made especially for the purpose of putting stuff on when we're working ritual. So technically, it's an altar. But it's more of a work table than place of worship. We don't do any bowing of the head and that sort of stuff there, at least, not when anyone's looking. We call upon the Ancestors every time we lay the compass. So they are an integral part of the compass. They define the shape and the texture of the crafting we do, and they're largely responsible for channelling the energies for us. We do everything indirectly through the ancestors to a certain extent. And of course the River of Blood, the current of the Tradition is made up from the memories and the energies of our ancestors.

Of course, an obvious way that we use our ancestral connections is in the technique of tapping the bone, or rather the series of techniques that come under the heading of tapping the bone. Tapping the bone is literally getting information from the ancestors, and trying to awaken some of those memories that lie dormant in our genes, in our cellular structure, in our blood and bone if you like. It is discussed in detail in the next section.

Recovering the lore is very important. Obviously, despite many grand claims to the contrary, you're not going to find an unbroken chain of Pagan practice stretching back from the modern day right through to pre-Christian Britain. You may find fragments here and there. You may find families that have kept some sort of esoteric practice going without really calling it Pagan or being Pagan in any way. And that's fine, that's cool, as long as it doesn't get misrepresented as being grander than it is. But you can take these pieces, these fragments that you can find out from research and from reading and studying, from talking to people, from working with people who've done that sort of thing, and picking up some hints and tips from them. And then you can take that to the ancestors themselves and work on filling in the gaps, recovering the lost lore, which is what a lot of people do.

We tend to reconstruct our traditions rather than inherit them these days. That doesn't make them any less valid. And it certainly doesn't make them any less potent, but acknowledging that fact does make them a lot more honest. I think that's a very important thing. Even where you do have somebody who has any sort of valid claim of stuff being handed down through generations however long, even they are generally in the situation where they are going to be recovering lore through tapping the bone in some way or another.

One of the really interesting things is that of course in ritual space the aim is to step outside of time for a while. When you're not in the mundane realm, you're really in the eternal now where past, present, and future meet. And so, one of the concepts that people find a little difficult to grasp, but it actually makes perfect sense when you think about it, although most people try not to, is that the ancestors aren't just the people who are from the past. We often refer to our ancestors as "ancestors past, and ancestors yet to be".

Those who come after us are also our ancestors. It helps to not be thinking in too linear a fashion when you start talking about stuff like that. Luckily when we're in the middle of one our rituals, being linear is generally the hardest thing to do. And so you can actually fall into that eternal nowness, the eternal state of becoming, which is so potent and powerful when it comes to working any sort of magic. Of course, in any talk about ancestors, you really can't leave out the oldest of ancestors. Many shamanic traditions — and the traditional crafting traditions of the British Isles are no exception here — think of the Gods themselves as being the most ancient ancestors. They see us humans as being part of that continuous line between the gods and modern man. And that's why we always consider that we're all sacred and we all have a divine spark within us. After all, there has to be something of worth within us. Otherwise, why would the ancestors talk to us?

Tapping the Bone

Many cultures around the world operate from a belief that the Gods are divine ancestors, from the Shinto religion in Japan, through many African traditions and the Maoris, to many of the Witchcraft Traditions of old Europe. For most of them, reverence for more mundane ancestors is also a major factor in their beliefs.

As a practitioner of the Elder Faith, ancestral workings are an integral part of my practice. Technically speaking, every time I commune with my Gods, I'm connecting with my ancestors on many levels, and I find a lot of satisfaction is to be had from working this way. The Tradition that I follow places great emphasis on connecting with the ancestors, and I can't think of a single working that doesn't involve them in some way.

Whenever we do a rite, we start by activating the altar. There are two essential things on our altar, the Stone and the Bone. The Stone is our hearthstone — the coven has one and many if not all of us have personal ones on our own altars too. It represents the hearth at which we gather — a strong family connection. It has other meanings too, but that is the primary one. The Bone is traditionally a skull, and in simpler times would have literally been the skull of an ancestor. For us it is more practical to use a beautiful life-size pewter skull, covered in Celtic knot-work. This represents the Ancestors, and when we activate the altar, part of it is to "breathe life" into the ancestors, that we may enflesh their legacy.

We always invite them to attend our rites, and at our initiations they are an essential component, as the candidate is first fostered into the family, and then later, when the ancestral memories have been shown to be active in them, adopted into the family as full members.

Our training is experiential — we learn by doing, and the exercises we do are designed more to awaken those ancestral memories than they are to teach us technique. We do use technique, but once the memories are awakened, we find that the tools that got us there often fall away to allow the inherent processes to take over.

We also seek to expand our understanding of Lore, and that is where tapping the bone comes in. Alongside our practical work, we make use of myth, poetic language and riddles to help us to uncover the underlying principles of our practice, for if we understand the principles, we can devise new or improved practical techniques. "Tapping the bone" refers to the act of tapping into the ancestral memories in order to work through these mythic, poetic or riddling concepts. It is a form of directed gnosis. The result of this is that the Tradition itself evolves, never static, always changing, as we discover new lore or reclaim lore that was lost.

Each of our initiates works with a Patron/Matron, a specific deity who chose us at our initiation/fostering. We work daily through devotions and meditations to deepen our link with our Patron, and our understanding of the Lore is coloured by the nature of that entity. We then share our individual perspectives in order to create a more rounded whole.

Sabbats for us revolve around our path, our Gods, and our ancestors. We do not use an agricultural Wheel of the Year, but rather the cycle of the Sacred King. As a result, we all walk the Wheel in a very real way — it has a profound effect on every aspect of our lives, and our Sabbats flow together as parts of a whole because of this. At Samhain, we work a public rite with Gwyn ap Nudd and the Wild Hunt, bringing the souls of those who died during the year together to be escorted through the Gates into the Cauldron of Rebirth, and a private working, where we explore the Mysteries of the Mound.

Part of our involvement in ancestral working is that we don't hold with the modern concept of reincarnation. We see the rebirth of individuals as a privilege, not a right. Most people when they die are returned to the Cauldron of Cerridwen, to become part of the cosmic "soup" from which all things are made. Whilst they live again, it is not as one discrete individual, but rather their components are recycled. However, there are those who, by some great deed of heroism, spirituality or wisdom, earn the right to come back as whole individuals. We call them the Mighty Dead, and they become teachers and leaders who come back again and again until they are ready to stop returning. These are the ancestors we work with, and learn from, and hope to become.

One last note on ancestors — believing, as we do, that time only appears to be linear, we see ancestors as being those who came before us, and those who come after us; ancestors who were, and who are yet to be. Working with ancestors requires an appreciation of paradox, for as the old Witch saying goes, "Truth is most oft found twixt the horns...."

Generally, books on Wicca don't speak much about ancestral work, and there is an unfortunate popular impression that one of the great differences between Wicca and Traditional Witchcraft is that Wiccans don't work with ancestors. This is not true. It may not be written about much, but from my years as an Alexandrian High Priest, I can tell you that while they work in a different way, the ancestors do play an important part for the Wicca as well. Traditional Witches often put down Wiccans as "Fluffy Bunnies" because they are generally more inclined to lighter, gentler practices, but Wicca is a tradition as valid as any passed on within a family for generations, and Gardner himself showed evidence of tapping the bone when he wrought his Wicca out of the pieces he was given by his initiators.

Likewise, Wiccans often put down Traditional Witches as being dark, even demonic, when the truth is that we all come out of the darkness, and the point of balance is where there is greatest power and beauty.

Dark and Light,
Black and White,
Witches crafting through the Night.

Reincarnation
Cosmic Soup and the Mighty Dead

There are a lot of different opinions about reincarnation. Many are loosely based on Hindu and Buddhist beliefs, while others are based on personal insights. One thing that most Neopagan ideas about reincarnation share is the idea of choosing whether or how you come back. The popular idea seems to be that when Joe dies, he will come back as Joe's spirit in another body. He won't remember being Joe, unless he is sufficiently spiritually enlightened to earn the right to remember, but the Spirit of Joe lives on intact and eternal.

For me, this is a very simplistic interpretation of the eastern philosophies, and not one I subscribe to at all. Among other things, I do past life regressions, so it usually comes as a surprise to people when they find out that I don't agree with the idea of a linear progression of lives for the individual. So what do I believe in?

First, let me state that I absolutely accept the concept of reincarnation, but for me it is mostly a case of recycling than the continuation of an individual. You see, my ancestors believed that when you died, you were placed in the Cauldron of Rebirth, and all that you were, body soul and spirit, returned to the Cosmic soup from which it came. New bodies, spirits and souls were created from this soup, so yes, you reincarnate, you come back, but not as one discreet individual. This has several important ramifications for me. Firstly, it means that the progress of the individual is of vital importance to the progress of humanity as a whole, because when you return to the soup, your level of enlightenment will raise or lower the overall level of enlightenment of the whole soup, just as the flavour of individual ingredients affect the overall flavour and quality of a mundane soup. Secondly, it is not a matter of choice. There is no more choice than there is concerning the breakdown of your physical components to return to the earth, be it by decomposition or by fire.

There are exceptions — the Mighty Dead. My ancestors also believed that there were individuals who became worthy, by acts of heroism, great spirituality, wisdom or leadership, to become one of the Mighty Dead, who do not return to the soup, but emerge from the Cauldron revitalized. These are the Great Teachers and Heroes, and they are rare but essential for the progress of the whole of humanity.

So why do I do past-life regression work, you might ask — well I also believe in ancestral memories. For me, the lives that are tapped into during the regression sessions are those we carry memories of in our blood, our bones, our genetic makeup. I've noticed patterns in the geographical placement of individual's "past lives" that suggest the migration of a family over the eons. This becomes of vital importance in the spiritual path I follow, where the aim is to recover and reconnect to the Lore of our ancestors. This approach has reaped dividends for me and those I work with.

This is also strongly connected to my attitude towards free will and destiny. I don't believe in free will, not because I subscribe to a concept of predestined actions that were set in stone at the beginning of time. I don't think anything is set in stone before it occurs, and all options are always open, but the decision we make at any given moment is the only decision we could make at that moment, for better and worse. Therefore, in the instant, there is no choice, no free will. We are bound to respond the way we do. But awareness of that enables us to overcome it. We cannot be other than who we are in the instant, but we can work to change who we are, so that our reaction is different because we are different. It is not an easy concept to grasp, because it is non-linear, and involves an awareness of the eternal now behind the illusion of Time. Thus we cheat Fate by surrendering to it, and working with it instead of against it. Walking the path of the Craft was never meant to be easy, and much of it involves reconciling apparently irreconcilable points of view, paradoxes. As an old saying goes, the Truth lies "betwixt the horns".

The concept of reincarnation involves paradox too. We are reborn through the Caldron, but who we are ceases to be. Yet by encountering our death and rebirth whilst still in the body, we can move towards the realm of the Mighty Dead, to ride with Gwyn ap Nudd on the Wild Hunt instead of being that which They hunt, the souls of the recently departed. It all sounds rather melodramatic, but it is just the cycle of life and death. Some Christians make a big deal about being born again, and some Pagan paths talk about being twice-born, but the deeper Mysteries refer to the Greatest among us as Thrice-Born or Thrice-Great, such as Hermes Trismegistus. First we are born of our mother, and then reborn of the Goddess, but that last step is the doozy — to be reborn of the Cauldron while still in the flesh… it takes wisdom, courage, and surrender.

Funnily enough, the concepts upon which the Neopagan and New Age ideas of reincarnation are built are actually closer to this idea of Cosmic Soup than you might think. Like many spiritual ideas, reincarnation was simplified for the masses by the gurus of the sixties, and the buffet-style spirituality of the 21st century embraces that simplicity. It isn't a bad thing, but there are some who look for deeper, darker fare, and that leads them down avenues that were never meant to be for everyone. To each according to their needs — all paths lead to the same destination, some are just longer, or harder, or take a more scenic route. When all's said and done, in this too, we merely do what we are fated to do... we do what is necessary.

Finding Lore

Perhaps the biggest difference between Traditional Crafting and the various neo-Pagan paths is that the Crooked Path is very invested in finding, enfleshing and experiencing Lore in a very direct way, while neo-Paganism tends to be more involved with ritual dramas re-enacting the Lore rather than experiencing it directly.

Poetry and Myth

Lore can be found in the myths and legends of the Gods and Goddesses of the Path. In our case, many of the stories and poems are to be found in the Mabinogion. There are many translations of this collection of stories, but we primarily use two. The recent translation by Siobhan Davies is probably the most complete and accurate translation, and I personally found it enlightening to read, as it gave me new insights into the heart of the stories. The other version is the translation by Lady Charlotte Guest — the original translation. It is not so accurate, linguistically speaking, but what it does retain very well is the poetry of the original.

Poetry is very important to the Traditional Crafter. We make our students struggle with the White Goddess because it helps us understand how to "think poetically". Poetry is the language of the gods, so it naturally follows that in order to interact with and understand our deities, we need to learn to think and communicate poetically.

Ancestral Memory

The key to Ancestral Lore lies in the Ancestral memory. It is generally believed by traditions that work with the Ancestors, that the memories, experiences and learning of our ancestors are locked into our blood, our DNA. As a result, we have a group of techniques and rituals that are designed to help us come to terms with that. We use a combination of the Tapping the Bone techniques already described, and direct interaction with the Ancestors in our rites.

Crown and Drake

Most traditions of magick refer to a Higher self and a Shadow self in some way. In our path, we have come to use the terms Crown and Drake, because of the way that we work with these aspects of our psyche. The Drake, or Dragon, is the shadow self, the part of us that dwells in the Wasteland or Underworld, while the Crown is that bright spark of humanity — our higher selves — that dwells with the Gods.

The effective crafting of magic involves awakening the dragon under the control of the crown, often depicted in heraldic form as a dragon with a crown around its neck, like a collar.

The Witch Mark

The Witch Mark is an interesting concept. It has existed for a very long time in literature and mythology, and a lot of interesting things have been said about it over the years. In literature, you often find the idea of the Witch's Mark being an extra nipple or teat often under the armpit that is used to feed your familiar or an imp or devil given to you by Satan.

Obviously, Witches are not really Satanic, so that really doesn't apply here. Witch Marks are also seen as, in some stories, as brand marks or marks of possession, like cattle brands, or natural deformities or blemishes on the skin, which show that you have the Witch's birth-right if you like. There's a whole range of things really, though most of it stems from the time of the Inquisition, when there was quite a trade in Witch-finding.

Matthew Hopkins, a famous Witch finder of England, the Witch-Finder General, and quite a large number of fellows of a similar nature, used to go around charging a penny a time — or in some cases a shilling a time — to identify Witches. They would do this by looking for the Witch's Mark.

According to the Inquisition, the Witch Mark was a mark that was placed on the body by Satan himself at the Witch's initiation, and it was frequently described as being a suckling place for the familiar or imp. But it was usually seen as a discoloration of some sort, or at least it started out that way, that was impervious to pain.

The way they used to search for it was by sticking pins in you. They had a particular type, a pin called a bodkin, which was a long sharp pin with a wooden handle. They would prod away at you until they found somewhere that you didn't feel any pain.

That's all well and good, except that you have to remember the fact that there are areas in the human body where the skin doesn't have that many pain receptors. So you can find points where you can stick a pin in without causing pain, even in a perfectly normal person. There are also lots of reasons why areas of insensitivity might arise, due to injury or illness, so there was plenty of opportunity for them to find what would be considered at the time as real Witch's Marks.

But you have to remember these guys were earning a living with this, and so they tended to hedge their bets a little. They would have trick bodkins, ones where they were able to allow the pin to retract into the handle to give the appearance of piercing the skin without causing any pain. As time went by, this became a very common practice. It was a good way to earn a living in those times, and there were always plenty of people willing to have a go.

So as you would expect, there were people being accused left, right, and centre during the time of the Inquisition. And the strangest things became referred to as Witch's Marks. There are actually some historical ones that are long standing. For example, the possession of an extra finger on one hand was seen as the mark of the Witch. Ann Boleyn was said to have six fingers on her left hand. And the left hand is of course significant here. And though she was never actually openly accused of Witchcraft, if I remember rightly, mainly because she was married to the king at the time, but certainly when she had her head removed from her shoulders, part of the reason was because she was considered to be a Witch.

But as time went by, pretty much any deformity or irregularity of the body could be referred to as a Witch's Mark, if the bearer of the unfortunate stigmata happens to have land that somebody else wanted or had somehow upset or annoyed somebody in some way. So pretty much anything could be considered the Witch's Mark at that point, it was all fair game for the sticking of fake pins into the body, and ending up at the gallows or on the bon fire if you were really unlucky.

So is there any significance to the Witch's Mark? Is there any basis in fact on it? Well, that really depends on who you talk to. Most Witches will say that there is not a physical mark that is placed on the body, but there is a spiritual mark that happens during your initiation, whether it is a spontaneous initiation that happens within, or the rite of passage into a coven or group. There is said to be a mark placed on your aura that all other Witches can see.

There is certainly something about someone who has undergone a true initiation. You certainly get a feeling that they might be "one of us" as it were. And so I'm inclined to believe it.

There are some traditions do practice more or less temporary markings in tandem with initiation. They may mark the Mark of Cain, which is of course another classic example of the Witch's Mark: a circle-cross or a crow's foot or goose foot somewhere on the body. Usually it is marked temporarily, but there are traditions that still do it permanently. In the old days, it would have been marked with a Blackthorn thorn — try saying that ten times fast — because the Blackthorn has rather a lot of bacteria on the thorn, and it was necessary to make use of what you'd learned by way of wort cunning, or herb lore, to prevent sickness or even death as a result from having your skin scratched by the very sharp Blackthorn. And it would always leave a scar. And that was really quite an effective way of doing it.

Nowadays, there are other ways to test herb lore skills, and so I doubt there's many groups, if any at all, who actually scratch you with a Blackthorn anymore. But there are other ways of marking, with the number of different groups and different traditions that are out there, pretty much every part of the spectrum is covered somewhere I would imagine.

So the Witch Mark, yes it does exist, has existed historically as a physical mark. Nowadays, it's more likely to be a metaphysical marking in the aura. Hollywood and the Spanish Inquisition made full use of it, took poetic license to the extreme and made it into something quite spectacular.

Red Blood and White

There has been a lot of discussion in the Pagan community lately about Witch Blood, the idea of whether a Witch is born or made. And there's a lot of people, especially younger solitary people, who are promoting the idea that they were born a Witch, and that they have the Witch Blood and that's the only real way to become a Witch.

Meanwhile, there are other people who are arguing that the only way to become a Witch is to train and initiate with a group. There's a lot of politics, and a lot of personal opinion, and a lot of bile, quite frankly, being exchanged from person to person, not in a good way I hasten to add, about this whole concept of Witch Blood.

It has been used in the past in arguments for and against traditional hereditary family trads. And bad blood, if you'll pardon the expression, was also evident in those arguments. Although they seem to have died down lately, nobody really has a claim to be fam-trad anymore. It's just not the done thing. Even the people who consider themselves to be fam-trad don't make public claims of that sort anymore.

But what exactly is Witch Blood? And why is there so much fuss about it? Well, part of the problem is that Witch Blood has made its way into literature, into fiction and television shows like the series Charmed. The idea that the "Charmed Ones" were born a special way, have this special DNA that is instilled in them at birth that makes them able to be the "Charmed Ones". Mere ordinary Wiccans cannot hope to become "Charmed Ones", or part of their coven, because they weren't born Witches. And this has entered into the fantasy life of people who would like to think they're Witches. Serious Witches tend not to make such a big deal about it, but there are a bunch of people out there who basically use the Witch-born idea as an excuse for why they don't have to read any books, or do any studying, or actually do any practical work at all. It's really quite sad.

I'm not speaking about everybody there, though. Everybody knows at least one person who's like that, who makes all the claims and backs it up with absolutely nothing, and this is a common theme where Witch Blood is concerned. However Witch Blood, like the Witch Mark has been around a lot longer than the modern Pagan online community. In fact, you could trace it back as far as the Sumerian and Babylonian myths with the Anunaki, and Enki and Enlil creating humanity.

Then there was Lilith and Lilitu and what eventually became the story of Adam and Eve in the Christian Bible — there really is quite interesting material in those myths, when you read that the first man was created, and then his children, his first children were actually not sired by Adam — the first man — but were rather sired by Enki upon the lady who became Eve, or in other versions of the story on Lilith.

These, the offspring of this union with Enki ended up being the Witch Blood, the Watchers — there are lots of different names for them, the overseers, even the vampires. In some stories they end up becoming the vampires of myth and lore. But whatever else you can say, there certainly seems to be a trend that was started by the Sumerians and the Babylonians. Another version of the Witch Blood story starts with Tiamat, the mother of dragons. And dragon blood is a very important metaphor for Witch Blood.

Of course, in Semitic realms, and in fact throughout Europe, it ended up that the Witches were the Children of Cain. Cain was marked because of killing his brother and he went off to the Land of Nod and lived with the non-Edenic people, and they ended up being the ancestors of modern Witches, so the storey goes, including the grandson of Cain, who was Tubal Cain, the first blacksmith.

Because of this, there's a lot of blacksmith lore tied up in Traditional Witchcraft. It's actually a very interesting thing to study, but it'll suck you in there. You'll be reading books, and perusing web sites, and visiting museums for years. Chasing this down is a fascinating subject.

Anyway further down the line, the Witch Blood, the divine blood if you like, makes its way into the Merovingian court, the Dragon Kings of Europe, who claimed Fairy origins, as well as the whole Holy Blood, Holy Grail thing with Mary Magdalene. I'm not going to bore you with the details of that. Just wait till the movie comes out, "The Da Vinci Code". And they'll fill you in with all the details. And I'll leave it up to you to believe what you want to believe.

I'm actually quite fond of the theory of JC and Mary Magdalene getting together and producing a "sprog", but that's because I'm strange, and things like that tickle my fancy. But we'll move swiftly on from that. The basic idea is that there is this strand of DNA, if you like, this genetic marker that makes you a Witch or doesn't. And most people would say bull, because nine times out of ten there's a... it's being implied that I am the one who has this and you don't. And so it's used in a very elitist way, a very silly way, by all arguments.

There is also the fact that if you go back far enough in time any DNA strand that was exclusive to one particular family will by now have been diluted through the entire human population. So chances are more likely than not that I have this Witch Blood DNA, and you have this Witch Blood DNA, and the person sitting next to you at work has this Witch Blood DNA, which is really quite depressing. Of course, theories have a habit of evolving, and I'm actually quite in favour of this.

I like the idea of there being this divine spark in our genetic make-up. And what the current way of looking at it is that we all have this spark, we all have the potential if you like. But the potential has to be awakened and that's easier to do in some people than in others. Just like recessive genes for hair colour and eye colour come and go and skip generations, so does the propensity to activate this particular genetic marker if you like, and wake up the Witch Blood.

Generally, you're looking at an experience like a life threatening experience, a traumatic experience or a carefully constructed initiatory experience within a training group to do this awakening. Or sometimes it can be spontaneous in those that are gifted or cursed, depending on your perspective. Basically, the idea is that, as Robert Cochran said - and has been quoted frequently by many people — "A Witch is born not made". Well, this is only half of the story. The full quote should be, "A Witch is born not made. But if a Witch is to be made, then tears must be shed beneath the moon light" or something like that.

Basically the idea is that you have to be both born, you have the natural inclination and propensity towards Witchcraft, but then that has to be triggered; it has to be woken up. You have to awaken the ancestral memories, and this is what the training and education within a coven or working group is all about.

Witch-blood, or the Ancestral line, is often described as the Red line or ribbon, and there is also mention of the White line or ribbon. These are basically terms that represent the Tradition's lineage, which is important internally, but not necessarily to the rest of the world. A White line, or white blood, refers to semen, or the seed, and represents a tradition that is being newly created or discovered, during which time it is usually called a Path. When a Tradition has three generations of practitioners — in other words the founding members have initiated students who have themselves initiated students — it becomes a Red line.

Herb Lore

I should warn you I'm about to have a little bit of a rant here, because if there's one thing that really drives me crazy it's the absolute crap that you can find about herb lore online. Please, please, do not take anything as gospel that you read on line about herb lore. I have read some of the most atrocious drivel that's supposed to be herb lore.

And the really scary thing is that a lot of the stuff that is really bad is medical herb lore. The last thing in the world you want to make a mess up on is medical herb lore. So please, use reliable sources when you're researching anything to do with herbs, whether it's for magical, medical, or beautician purposes. Just make sure that your source is reliable. Don't pay any attention to some of the crap that you'll find on line. Some people are so irresponsible with their web sites; it really, really concerns me.

On that subject, let's talk a little bit about healing herbs. Now, I am not going to recommend any herbs for medical conditions, and I heartily recommend that you do the same — Ok? The important thing to remember here is that if you diagnose or treat illnesses when you are not a medical qualified practitioner, there's two things that you're leaving yourself wide open to. Number one is you're leaving yourself wide open to be sued by the person that you're advising, because you're not qualified to give them that advice. If it turns out to be not beneficial to them, guess what? They can sue your ass.

The other thing you're also leaving yourself wide open to is some time in jail, because guess what — it is an offense to impersonate a medical practitioner. And that's what you're doing. You're playing doctor. So don't do it, unless you have a medical qualification, do not diagnose or treat any illnesses from anybody. Now you may be a member of a coven or group where they say otherwise. Well, that's between you and your coven. I don't want to know.

But I'm saying, my advice to you is if you want to play around with the medical use of herbs, practice on yourself, because you're not likely to sue yourself. And they're not likely to arrest you for practicing on yourself either. Otherwise, we'd all be in trouble. So should you want to look into healing herbs for your own personal use, remember, don't go by some of the crap that's out there on the internet.

My suggestion is to stick to a good reliable source such as "A Modern Herbal" by Grieve. It's pretty much the best of the herbal books, and it's pretty cheap as well, if you buy it on Amazon or at your local metaphysical book store. You should always support your local Pagan businesses, of course.

"A Modern Herbal" by Mrs. Grieve is really, really a very, very good book, and I heartily recommend also getting a book called "A Herbal Medicine Maker's Handbook" by Green, which has a little bit of the medical herb lore in it, but more importantly, it tells you what to do with the herbs, how to make your teas, your poultices, your creams, lotions, etc., out of the herbs once you've decided what you want to use. It's a really good book. It's a lot of fun, and it tells you how to do everything with everyday bits and pieces you'll find in the kitchen rather than buying expensive laboratory equipment. Not quite as efficient, but a damn sight cheaper and a lot of fun as well.

I use a cream that I make myself for eczema on my hands. It's a recipe that my brother gave me. He is a qualified medical practitioner, and he teaches naturopathy, aromatherapy, reflexology, and acupuncture in Canada. His name is Colin Paddon if you ever come across him, in Ontario. He's really good at what he does. And he's a great healer as well. Just a little plug for my brother, in case he's listening. In the lotion that I make, I use the herbs that he told me to use, and I make them up using the recipe that's in the "Herbal Medicine Maker's Handbook". It is brilliant, a really nice moisturizing cream basically, that works wonders for my cracked skin.

So check out those two books if you want to do the herbal medicine route. And obviously the best way to do that is to actually go get qualified as a medical herbal practitioner. Courses are very expensive, and they're difficult to find. But there are some really good ones out there. So, it's worth the trouble if that's what you're interested in.

Of course, if you're like me, your interest in herbs is more likely to be involved in using them magically. And there are a couple of different ways you can do that. You can use them in incense, of course, and you can also use them in Mojo bags, and other nefarious and interesting ways. We're going to talk a little bit about a few of those.

I'm not going to be too specific because the herbs you use magically tend to be down to correspondences for the tradition that you follow, and obviously, you might not follow the same sort of tradition that I do, so any correspondences I give you may not be particularly useful. Most tables of correspondences tend to work on a planetary setting, so that's a good place to start. But you may work Qabalistically, in which case the spheres of the Tree of Life would be your focal point. Or you may work in some other system completely.

The important thing is that you have a table of correspondences where this herb corresponds with that event or that energy, and so on and so forth with that deity, and that will help you decide what herbs to use magically.

Using them in incense is pretty straight forward — you make an interesting blend. One of the things that often gets left out when people are making their own incense, try and work with the quantities that you're using in such a way that you end up with something that not going to make you cough and choke in the middle of your ritual. Something that smells half way decent is always a good idea.

There's actually a really simple way of working this. The trick here is that you start off by having a bowl with some coffee grounds in by your side. What you do is you take the ingredients that you've decided need to go into this incense, and you start off by getting an idea of what they smell like individually by having a charcoal block burning, and you put a little bit, and it really has to be a little bit, you don't pile the stuff on — I mean literally just a pinch — and hold your nose over it and waft into your nostrils and see what it smells like.

In between each ingredient, what you should do is take a good sniff of the coffee grounds, because that clears your nasal palate so you don't get any left over from the previous scent while you smell the current scent. It's a little trick from the fragrance industry which somebody once shared with me, and it really does work well.

Once you've familiarized yourself with the scent of each individual ingredient, you then want to decide what your main ingredient is going to be and then start experimenting. The trick here is to play with different quantities. Don't just put an equal amount of each in and expect it's going to smell lovely. For example, if you're doing a horned god incense, you might want to start off with oak moss because it's got that nice rich earthy forest smell to it, and it's really, really quite strong. That might be half of your recipe, just the oak moss, and then you might want to put something else in.

You've got earthy and mossy and foresty there, but you want to sweeten it up a little bit. So maybe a little tiny bit of mistletoe oil added to the oak moss would be really cool, and in that way you just sort of tweak things until you get a scent that's really pleasing, and really says to you what it is you want the incense to be used for.

The other trick is to try and have at least one of the ingredients as an essential oil. The reason for this is that it'll make sure it burns more smoothly, and you'll also get a lot more smoke from the incense, which of course is the point of burning incense — to get nice wafts of smoke that smell pretty, drifting around in the temple. So having at least one ingredient as an oil, is usually a pretty good idea. Also, try not to over-do the resin. Resin is really cool stuff, but if you have too many resins in your recipe, you end up with a sticky mess on your charcoal, which doesn't work at all. So, you want have something that is herb, that is leaf or wood or stem and use that as a base, and then have some resin, some oil and then work on from there.

What you get then, is that there is a nice incense because you've balanced scents together. It smells good. It evokes the energies of what it is that you want to use it for, and you've also got a good texture thing going which gives you different types of smoke, so it tends to burn for longer and smoke for longer as well. You end up with a very well-crafted incense, and people will be absolutely amazed. So that's the secret tips to incense making.

To make a Mojo bag? You use exactly the same herbs, but you throw them in a cotton bag to use as a sort of herbal talisman. You might throw a few semi-precious stones in there, obviously sticking to the correspondences again, and away you go. So it's really quite simple. I'm not going to dwell on that one too much.

Another way of using herbal ingredients magically is — this might sound really silly, but — dressing your altar. There's an old ritual I use occasionally for consecrating a magical ring. It's from the Greek Magical Papyri, so it's a couple of thousand years old now. One of the things it does, it uses laurel leaves to dress the altar. You basically have your bowl of oil that you're going to use to consecrate that ring, and you surround it with laurel leaves. It's basically symbolic value there. And you can do stuff like that with dressing your altar, dressing your shrine, dressing the temple for that matter.

Making a wreath to hang behind your altar for the Sabbat is a nice way of using herbs in a magical way. So you know, ingenuity and imagination is the key here. Stick with your correspondences. Stick with what your tradition says is appropriate for the season or for the working and away you go. It's as simple as that.

Then of course there is one of the areas of use of herbal lore in magic that has be approached rather carefully and that is herbs and trance states. It is possible to give your trance states a boost and remain total legal. I know the wonders of hashish are well documented, but there's actually stuff that is much better to use magically, mainly because it doesn't end up invoking jail cells around you.

Perhaps the most commonly used trance inducing herb you'll find is mugwort. Mugwort is really good. You can put a little bit into your incense and it becomes a dream inducing or astral projection inducing or path working incense extraordinaire. The trick is to not over do it. Too much mugwort is going to leave you feeling very stupid. And you can get psychologically hooked on it as well. So use it sparingly. You don't want to sort of throw a fist full of mugwort on the charcoal block and just stick your head over it. That would not be a good thing. So mugwort I can heartily recommend, but you have to take it a little carefully. Use it in moderation, like all things, and you'll find it will enhance your trance work, it'll enhance path workings, journey work, anything of that nature. Also, oracular work, divination, it's very good for that.

For visionary stuff, if you use it properly salvia divinorum1 is very good, also known as diviner's sage. You can actually get that from a lot of places. The best thing to do is find somebody who can give or sell you a plant and grow your own, because that way you can guarantee the purity.

NOTE: Salvia Divinorum has been made illegal in several states. Check to make sure it is legal where you live.

One of the really cool things about Salvia Divinorum is that, they haven't found a toxic level for it yet. You can ingest a wheel barrow load of the stuff without any harm. They reckon that if there is a toxic level, you're going to fall asleep in a stupor before you'll hit the point where it's actually starting to do you any harm.

Now, taking Salvia Divinorum the traditional way is little tricky because it involves wedging a huge amount of leaf into your mouth, chewing it and letting the saliva and juice gather under your tongue. It's really unpleasant, it's really bitter. Some people might like it, I personally can't stand it.

You can buy salvia leaves that have been treated with a concentrated extract. I'm not really into that. It's not really the natural approach. You can also smoke it. My favourite way of using it is you can get these vaporizers that are actually sold for people who are using medical marijuana. It is like a little pipe, and has a little burning plate. You can finely chop your salvia and vaporize it on the plate, and that actually works incredibly well. It's a lot healthier than smoking it in a roll up, because you usually have to cut it with tobacco to make that work. So you're avoiding the tobacco.

You're actually avoiding hot smoke which can do damage to the tissue of your lungs, because the vaporized leaf, the vapour that you actually inhale, is only slightly warmer than room temperature by the time you inhale it. So it actually is a lot healthier for you. So if you're going to do it, do it that way. The other option is doing it the old fashioned way, the bitter leaf under the tongue. And you have to sort of keep it there for about fifteen minutes, chewing every now and then, trying not to drool green liquid everywhere. It can be messy. So that's Salvia Divinorum.

Perhaps my all time favourite is wormwood, which is a little tricky to use. Basically, what you want to do with wormwood is you want to take absinthe. Now there's a slight problem with absinthe in that it is not legal to make or sell absinthe in this country, although you can import it from overseas if you do so quietly. They don't like you bringing it over in large quantities, but you can buy a bottle of it from London and such places.

You can actually do a better job in most cases if you make your own. Obviously, you can't distil your own absinthe, but you can get a reasonable approximation. If you get a decent vodka and some good quality wormwood as well — once again it's best to grow your own, but you can buy dried wormwood if that's all you can get your hands on. The fresh stuff is so much better though, believe me. If you get one of the larger bottles of Smirnoff vodka, blue label is stronger than red label remember. And the stronger it is, the better it's going to work.

You basically take a small fist-full of wormwood and about an equal quantity of mint or lemon balm, and if you can throw some star anise in as well, that really helps. And what you do is you leave it in the bottle. You should probably transfer it into a mason jar so you've got the wide neck, it makes life a little easier. You put a fist-full of mint, a fist-full of wormwood, and maybe half a dozen star anise capsules, you know those little star shaped things into the big bottle's worth of vodka and give it a good shake at least once a day. And leave that for seven or eight days. And then you're good to go. You strain out all the herby bits, and you should have a nice green liquid at this point.

If you were allowed to legally distil it, you would then distil that, and then take a second bunch of mint leaves and wormwood and steep that in the distilled liquid for another seven days and then strain it again. That would be real absinthe. But without the distillation, you can get a perfectly useable beautiful green liquid that has all the properties. It's not quite as smooth. It's not quite as tasty as the distilled product, but it will do the job quite nicely. What you do is you mix it 50/50 with water.

If you're really lucky and if you've used fresh ingredients, you will find that if you drizzle iced water through a sugar cube instead of just mixing it, you will actually get the louche effect where the liquid goes from a clear emerald green to an opaque milky greenish white. And that's really quite magical by itself.

Absinthe has a wonderful effect of giving you a very clear headed intoxication that is very good for artistic endeavours and for magical work. That's why it's my favourite. Also, if you do it to that recipe which is very close to the original Henri Pernod recipe, the stuff that Toulouse-Lautrec used to drink, it actually tastes pretty darned good too. So that's what I'm going to leave you with, how to make a legal substitution for absinthe that will make a wonderful pre-ritual tipple. Just remember, don't over indulge, because it helps to be reasonably in control of your faculties when you're trying to do a rite.

Tools

There are four tools that are basic to each individual's participation in the Work, and four tools that are basic to the group as a whole. The latter are:

The Stang

This is either a forked branch of suitable size, or a two-tined pitchfork. It represents Old Hornie, and is the True Altar of the Working, but in addition it represents the World Tree, by whatever name it is known in the tradition. This is the great Cosmic Axis, upon which hangs the Three Realms of Heaven, the Mundane World, and the Underworld, or "Heaven, Hell and Here", as we like to say. As the one cosmic structure that straddles all of the realms, it also becomes our bridge, and a frequent depiction of the initiate is as a squirrel or mouse, scurrying from world to world upon the Tree.

The Cauldron

A proper iron cauldron is used for containing the Balefire, for works of divination, and as a representation of the Grand Dame. Sacred to Cerridwen, this is the famed Cauldron of Rebirth, and as such it represents both the Womb and the Tomb. In fact, in our sacred space, you can see it in both functions... upright in the Northwest as the womblike Cauldron of Ced, and upturned in the Southeast as the tomb — like the topsy-turvy Bilé Tree, they are the opposite of what you would expect.

The Hearth-Stone

The true heart of the group, this stone represents our place at the Hearth of the Ancestors, and it is upon this stone we pledge our oaths. As the hearth-stone is the Heart-Stone of the coven, it carries much of the symbolism found associated with the Corner Stone in Christianity, but it is the most primitive form of the Altar of Offering, or of Sacrifice, and also the place where the most sacred activity of all is undertaken, the tending of the Sacred Flame.

The Skull

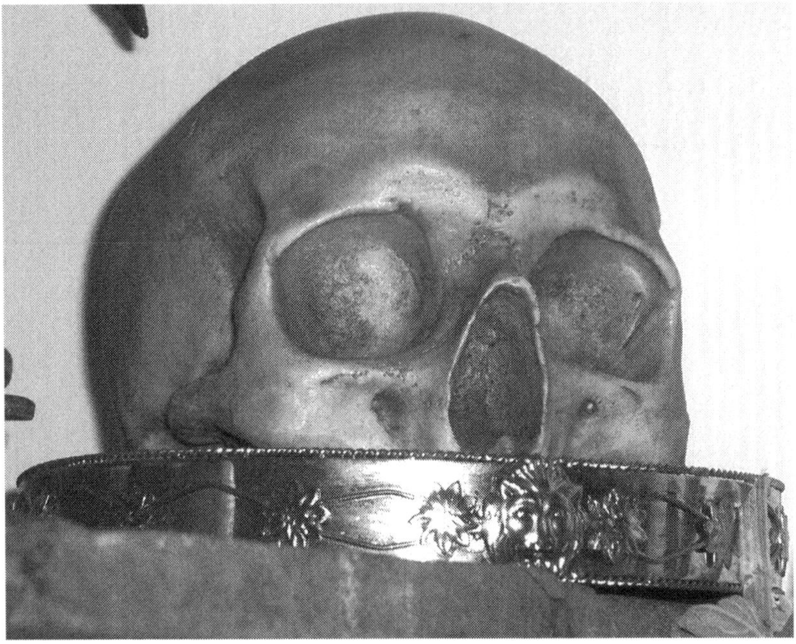

The skull both represents the Ancestors, and acts as a conduit for their participation in our work. It can be a real skull, or a representation of one, and like the Hearth-Stone should be treated with the utmost respect. Skulls have been associated with ancestor-worship from the dawn of humanity, and much of the fear and discomfort modern people feel around skulls is connected with an almost instinctual reverence for what they are, and what they represent. The human skull is also another form of Cauldron, this time containing treasures in the form of wisdom and understanding.

The personal tools are:

The Horn Cup

This is a stirrup cup of the type used by English Fox Hunts to toast the hunt, or a literal horn cup, made from a cow's horn. Each person may choose the animal that the cup is modelled on, the stag being recommended for those without a preference. It is used in the Houzle (The Red Meal, or sacrament of the Ancestors), and also used in the preparation of the elixirs. It may be made of horn, of pewter, or silver. Brass, while traditionally acceptable, is not practical for use with alcohol.

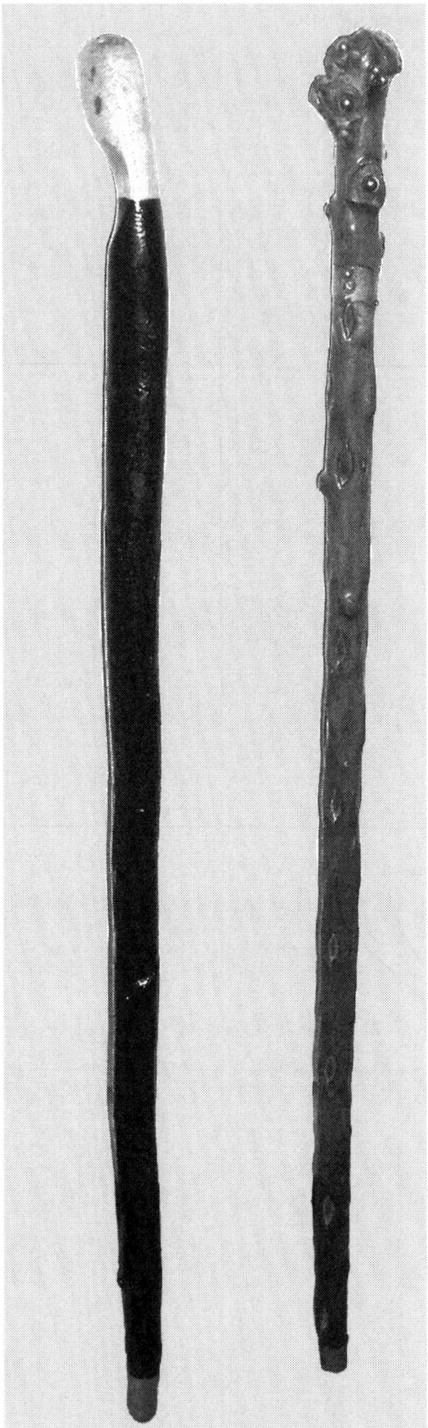

The Cane

A walking stick or cane of blackthorn is the traditional badge of the Cunning Folk, along with the horn cup. Master Crafters may carry a cane of blackthorn or other wood associated with their group to use as a blasting rod, and for other uses as become apparent to them.

The Cord

This is from most ancient times the mark of the Priesthood, a red cord wrapped about the left wrist or neck. It is found in the Mysteries of Ancient Egypt, and from there was adopted by the practitioners of the Qabalah, and its use was rumoured among the Bards of Britain. Our group uses a cord knotted in certain ways, to remind us of the bond of our oath, our connection to the Hearth-Stone, and our commitment to our Patron and Matron.

Of these tools, the Cup and the Cord are required upon admittance as a member of the group, so both Apprentices and their Mentors carry these. The Cane is carried by the Master Crafters, though the Apprentice may work with one from time to time.

The Giving of Gifts

In the Cunning Art, the giving and receiving of a gift has special significance. As for our Celtic ancestors, the giving of a gift implies an obligation on the part of the giver, that they are responsible for the recipient in some way. Likewise, the accepting of a gift is the acceptance of the authority of the giver over the receiver. When you give somebody a gift, you place them under your authority, and you are responsible for their protection and welfare. This is offset when gifts are mutually exchanged as a celebration. Thus it is appropriate that upon acceptance into the group, the new Apprentice should receive their cord from the hand of the one/s who initiate them, and their first horn cup from the one who becomes their Mentor.

The Cane should be procured by the member for themselves. However, if a gift is made of the Cane, it must be balanced by the exchange of a gift of value in return, for it is a mark of independence

— there is still a bond of service, but the assumption of the role of Master Crafter carries its own mantle and bonds directly to the Ancestors, and strengthening the ties to mentors and initiators is contrary to the intent.

Encountering the Crooked Path

For those walking the Crooked Path, the biggest issue is finding more material. Much like Wicca was, back when I first started to explore my spiritual path. There are very few books dealing directly with the subject, especially for the beginner. More advanced students can make use of some of the academic works, but the newcomer is left in the dark. That is part of the reason for writing this book, but there are sources that can be utilized by the seeker, providing they learn to make use of the particular mindset that this path engenders.

By a Bent Line, By a Straight Line, By a Crooked Line

This is a saying that is frequently heard from practitioners. It refers to the mindset required when walking the path, but it also describes the classic Witch's Mark, which is often depicted as a circle cross, but is more accurately portrayed as a Goose-Foot inside a circle.

As a description of the mindset used when walking upon the Crooked Path, it is an oblique reference to the description given to the candidate standing at the entrance to the temple, waiting to be initiated into the Ancient Egyptian Mysteries: "Behind you, the path twists from side to side, like a serpent, and before you it rises and falls like the waves of the sea. But beneath your feet, the path is straight and true, and you walk it with a firm step." This gives us a sense of a path that is not fixed or tied to a dogmatic approach, but rather one that shifts and turns with our growing and changing understanding of its nature. It is pinned to a specific meaning or way of being by us — we pin it to the mundane world and make sense of it "in the moment", but are aware that it has changed from what we thought it was yesterday, and we know that new insights will cause it to change tomorrow.

Truth Betwixt the Horns

The old saying "truth lies betwixt the horns" is a key one for the Crafter who is feeling their way along the path, because it refers to the flaming torch of enlightenment that burns between the horns of Auld Hornie, or as depicted in Eliphas Levi's painting of Baphomet. This is the key to a recurring puzzle in traditional crafting, that truth is often found in the resolution of paradox.

We often encounter this in the description of Gods and other entities we encounter. Goda is described as "neither black nor white, neither clothed nor naked, neither riding nor walking". This is often explained by the fact that she is partly in shadow (composed of both dark and light), wears a fishing net, and rides a goat with her feet trailing on the ground. But the key is really that the answer embraces fully both of the opposite things. Paradox is resolved when you find the point where the two opposites can both be true.

Do What is Necessary

Wiccans follow the Rede ("An it harm none, do as you will") and Christians follow the Ten Commandments. These are both moral codes, instruction on how to live a good life, and as such are ideally suited to help the average person navigate the morally ambiguous waters of real life.

But the traditional crafter is not average. The duty of the Crafter is to cheat Fate, to take responsibility for their own lives and actions, and so the Crafter follows an ethical code, best expressed by Robert Cochrane in the phrase "Don't do what you desire: Do what is necessary."

Morals tend to operate as absolutes — killing is immoral, as is theft. But in real life things are rarely so cut and dried. You may find yourself stealing bread to feed your starving child, or killing an intruder before they kill or rape your family. Then your theft and murder become "lesser evils", and you are ethically justified in these actions for the greater good.

The downside of this is that you are left with the need to constantly make decisions on the right course of action, rather than blindly operate in accordance with the inflexible moral code — the latter leads to zero tolerance and blind obedience, both of which are anathema to a true crafter. An ethical stance means constantly wrestling with the dilemma of what is the right thing to do, but it is worth it, because in taking full responsibility for your actions and decisions, you claim your place within the Ancestral Landscape, and you take a firm, resolved step towards being able to work powerful magic.

The Sacred Marriage

The Sacred Marriage, or Hieros Gamos, is depicted in many myths throughout the world. In ancient cultures it was manifest as a literal marriage ceremony, where the ruler was united with the earthly representation of Sovereignty in the form of a Priestess (Cult of Ishtar/Astaroth/Innana), a Queen of royal blood (Egypt), a horse (Epona, Ireland), and so on. But for the practicing Witch or Crafter, the Sacred Marriage is an entirely internal affair, at least on the personal level.

While the Hieros Gamos is a popular way of celebrating Beltaine, it is an outward expression of the inner process of uniting and balancing the Higher and Lower aspects of the self — the Drake and Crown or shadow and stellar selves. It is an act of completion that when fully expressed provides the third rebirth of the initiate, making them Thrice Great or adept.

Awen

In the Welsh Celtic Mysteries, Awen is the Divine Inspiration that emanates down to humanity from the Gods on high. Its three rays are said to represent land, sea and sky, or mind, body and spirit, or love, wisdom and truth. It is also the image of the first three sacred Coelbren letters given to Einigen Gawr, forming the basis of both the Secret Coelbren and the regular written Coelbren. These letters are said to be I, O, and U.

For the crafter, things go a little deeper, for just as there are three rays coming down from the Source Above, for crafters there are also three rays going up from the Source Below, and together these two Awen symbols form the Hex Star that is the simplest, truest symbol of the Craft.

In Place of Hierarchy

There's been a lot said over the years for and against joining a coven. Many people who choose to be solitary do so after a bad encounter with a Coven. Now sometimes they were unlucky enough to find a Coven that was not a good place to be, and sometimes the things that put them off were the very things that attract others.

Bad covens come in many shapes and sizes, but there are good ones too. What constitutes a bad coven? They usually fall into one of three categories. The first category is the "Look at me" coven. The members, especially the leaders, are so busy making a splash in the community, that there is no time for any real spiritual exploration. Either the posturing at public events consumes them, or they put the coven's activities on hold to play Media Witch at every opportunity. Usually — but not always — the fault lies with the leadership, as they set the tone. Symptoms: they host at least as many public rites as they do private ones, and progression is usually linked to the ability to perform in public. They will often accept and initiate all comers, as the size of the coven is an important status symbol. The leadership can often appear to be extremely knowledgeable, though often they only grasp the surface impression of the things they supposedly know.

The second category is the "Wanna-Be" coven, where there is often only a superficial level of knowledge and understanding, and rituals tend to be empty reconstructions of "how it was done" way back when. These rites can be quite beautiful as works of theatre, but have no depth or energy to them. They are often organized like a pageant, with committees splitting up the work. The phrase "wanna-be" is politically charged, of course. There's nothing wrong with being a "wanna-be" pagan. Technically, all of us who were not born of Pagan parents started out as a "wanna-be" as the first step to actually being Pagan. But for an entire coven to be "wanna-be", that is a tragedy. Usually the founders/leaders either decided one day to start a coven (not necessarily bad by itself, mind you), or tried joining a group and left to form their own because they thought they could do better themselves (again, not bad by itself). They typically do not have a great depth of knowledge or any real training, so they focus on the form of their rites rather than the Lore and Myth that should dwell as a living flame within the ritual structure.

The third category is more like a cult than a coven. Strictly controlled, they tend to be of the "one true and only way" variety. Often they are a "heretical" offshoot of a respectable Tradition, following their leader's personal understanding of the Trad. They are hard to join — or at least give that impression — and even harder to leave.

But there are things that, while they might not be to everybody's liking, are not the sign of a bad coven. For starters, the one that seems to be the biggie at the moment: covens who do not admit everyone who knocks on their door are not necessarily being elitist. In a small group practicing magick, it is important that newcomers fit in with the existing members, so there is at the very least going to be a check for compatibility. Some covens do it up front, some let a wider group in as dedicants and then filter out those who don't fit before they reach initiation. It is a common misconception that anyone can be a Witch or a Wiccan, but this path is not for all, just as Christianity, Buddhism and all the other religions are not meant to be for everyone. If you don't resonate to the Path, you should look for a different one.

There are covens out there that are very good at some things and lacking in others. For example, I know of a coven that excels at basic training. They train and initiate people, giving them a good grounding in what they need to be an effective Witch, but after that there is nothing — they go right back into the basic training cycle with a fresh batch of "newbies". Other covens might not handle newcomers so well, but are an excellent place for experienced Witches to come together and explore the deeper Mysteries.

Sometimes people think of a coven as a lifetime commitment, but that commitment is to the Path, not to any group of people. Technically, though there is usually a bond of initiation within a coven, it is in reality a group of solitary Witches whose paths happen to coincide for a while. All Witches should be practicing their art solo whether they are in a coven or not.

As you might have guessed, I'm a pro-coven person. So far I have worked solo for five or six years at a stretch on two occasions. I've trained with an Alexandrian coven in London (left due to misplaced loyalty to a friend who left in a huff), an eclectic coven (left because the leaders became media whores — even good covens can go bad, and vice versa), and two Traditional Witchcraft covens… I left one because it was that "basic training" coven, and the other because my path ceased to coincide with that of its leaders. Now I run a small coven with my wife. Some would consider us elitist because we are very picky about whom we let in — or even circle with. But part of that is to make sure we don't grow too fast for our own good. It is the second coven I've led, as I was HP of a Wiccan coven in the UK for about ten years before I came to the US.

So the short version of this story is that not all covens are good, but neither are all covens bad. Some benefit from coven interaction, and some are definitely meant to remain solitary. But the important thing is, whichever side of the fence you find yourself on, don't dismiss the possibility that things might change. Be open to exploring the opportunities that present themselves, and don't rule them out because of a prior bad experience. To quote a classic quote, "above all, to thine own self be true."

One of the things often quoted as a reason for steering clear of covens is the idea of hierarchy. In many modern covens, the leaders have absolute authority, and there is a definite pecking order. This is in itself not a bad thing, but it can easily get out of hand if there are not checks and balances to keep it in line. Many turning to a Pagan path after being left unfulfilled by Christianity rebel against any kind of hierarchy, and I have personally experienced serious abuse of the coven hierarchy in the past.

But magic and the Mysteries are not democratic, and cannot be effectively worked by consensus and the popular vote — at least, not in the long term. So my group has chosen to adopt the model used by medieval craft guilds, which are probably the original model for coven structure anyway. In this model, the leaders are "first among equals", and while they definitely rule, they rule by the consent of the members. This means that they can be removed if they get out of hand.

There are no set rules about structure, but we have a simple one based on experience:

The Dedicant

A student who has sought, and obtained, provisional entry into the Company. Characteristics are a dedication to learning, a hunger for knowledge, and a willingness to be open to possibilities. Responsibilities are to study, to attend workings where invited, and to demonstrate their readiness to move on to the stage of Apprentice.

The Apprentice or Squire

A student who has proven their connection to the Current, who has enflamed the blood, and been accepted as an apprentice by a Master Crafter, as a full member of the Company. Apprentice refers to one who is reliant on their Master for guidance and training, while squire refers to one who is more advanced, who is able to operate under their own steam, but is still answerable to their Master or Mistress. Responsibilities are to attend all gatherings of the Company (unless with good reason), to study and practice the Art as guided by their Master/Mistress, and to be silent on matters of the Art to all save full members of the Company.

The Master Crafter

An accomplished Crafter who has demonstrated that their apprentice days are behind them, who has enflamed the blood and summoned the ancestors — and who the ancestors have claimed as one of their own. All Master Crafters are equal in status, though one may consult or seek the advice of another as peer, and the relationship with the Crafter who was their Master/Mistress in the apprentice stage will probably remain a special one bound by mutual respect. Responsibilities are to participate fully in the Work of the Company, to study and practice their Art, and to find and mentor at least one Apprentice in their life. They are also required to participate in the choosing of leaders, and to serve as leader if chosen.

In addition, there are three roles within the group beyond that of member in good standing, the Magister, the Mistress, and the Guardian.

The Magister and the Mistress

The Magister and/or the Mistress lead the Company by the will of the members. They are to be chosen from those with great experience, and should demonstrate the qualities of leadership. They may be removed at any time by consensus of the Master Crafters. The term of office is seven years, after which the Magister, Mistress or pair must step down, and a new leader or leaders be chosen. The outgoing leaders may be selected to lead again, by consensus of the Master Crafters, but they must make offering before doing so. When the group selects a leader, the one chosen may not refuse, except for reasons of health or work commitments.

The responsibility of the Leader or Leaders is to set the pace of the group, having the final say on matters of training, practice and direction. They should set the schedule for group workings and classes in consultation with the members of the Company, and be the final arbiter in any matters where there is no consensus, and they should represent the group at larger gatherings where appropriate. But their authority ends there. Leaders may not place undue restrictions upon the personal life of members; they should not exercise their role in a commanding way, but rather act as first among peers, and lead by guidance and example. They pay the coin for all workings performed by the group, and so have final say in those workings.

The Guardian

Also known as the Black Rod or Summoner, the Guardian is chosen by the Leader or Leaders to perform a role that includes the following:

Ensuring that the place of working is secure, so that there are no distractions or intrusions;

Ensuring the well-being of the members participating, without interfering with their process unnecessarily;

Facilitating the needs of those running the working, providing they do not jeopardize the well-being of the participants;

Bringing matters of an ethical nature to the attention of the leader/s, over-ruling them where ethical concerns exist;

Representing the group in wider gatherings;

Representing the Leader/s when interacting with other groups;

Reminding members of their ethics where necessary.

The Guardian should not interfere with the private life of any member, except where it has a direct and significant impact on the group, and should not attempt to direct any member ethically outside of workings — in everyday life, members are free to make their own mistakes, learn their own lessons, and pay their own coin. In some groups the roles of Guardian and Summoner are held by different people.

Leaving

It is always within the rights of a member to take their leave of the group, to be released from all obligations to walk their path separately. A member who is a Master Crafter may elect to start a new group, and so long as the new group follows the same basic outline, it will be recognized as a sister-group. If a Master Crafter leaves for whatever reason, if they have an apprentice, that apprentice may choose to stay or leave with their mentor. If the apprentice chooses to stay, then a new mentor will be found for them — if there is nobody available without a current apprentice, this is an exception to the guideline that a Master Crafter should only have one Apprentice at a time, which is recommended to discourage too fast a growth of the group, and encourage discernment in who is accepted for training. Other circumstances that would warrant this are, for example, when someone approaches the group who is so obviously meant to be a part of it that to turn them away would be a crime against the Ancestors.

Karma or Fate

So I guess the thing we really need to do is to start off by talking about just exactly what karma is. For the average neo-pagan, Wiccan, or western adherent to some vague sort of Hindu faith, karma is more about what goes around comes around. To quote one of my favourite characters from the Victorian novel Water Babies, "Do as you would be done by and be done by as you did." from the teacher lady who's actually two characters. But then when have I ever been able to count?

This is probably best described as a very, very simple way of looking at cause and effect, and it extends into the realm of reincarnation. Karma and reincarnation in the mind of the average neo-pagan are very closely aligned, because karma is said to extend beyond this lifetime and into the next. You can be working through karmic debt from a previous lifetime in this one, so it's very confusing.

With it being so tied up with reincarnation, I guess we had better take a quick look at reincarnation too. Now the popular concept of reincarnation made very popular by all the Llewellyn books and by various other modern day publications, documentations, web sites, and television programs is the idea that everybody when they die, they get a little vacation in Summerland, and then they get to choose a body to be reincarnated in. They come back to the mundane realm as another person. And somewhere in the process of getting into that other person, they have their memory of their former lives erased, and so they can start again from scratch.

But they have a set of lessons that they've chosen to learn in this particular lifetime, and it has some interesting ramifications. For example, if you follow this doctrine of reincarnation, then suicide is a big, big no-no, because the doctrine doesn't really treat suicides very nicely. The basic concept is that if you commit suicide to get out of some issue in this life, then in the next life you'll be put back to deal with exactly the same issue, but you'll have it a little bit harder. So, it's probably a good idea to stick around and try and get it right the first time. Heh, heh. That's just me being evil.

The biggest problem with this concept of reincarnation is that it's been heavily polluted by western modes of thought, that says that everybody has the right to be whatever they want to be, and all men are created equal, and so on and so forth. Now technically speaking, all men are created equal, but, it doesn't stay that way for very long, because we all have different abilities and different problems, and that makes us all pretty unique and we're not all the same. That's something we should be all very grateful for.

Likewise, we don't all automatically get the right to reincarnate. When you actually look at the real concept of reincarnation, as practiced by the Hindus, it's a lot more complicated than that, because the idea of reincarnation in the Hindu faith is much more to do with recycling than being born again as it were. The concept is that when we die, the essence of who we are and what we are gets basically put into this huge melting pot, and becomes part of a cosmic soup from which ladles of new humanity are poured forth. And so, whilst we do get to come back, we don't get to come back as a single entity.

The idea is that we just get recycled, which is an interesting concept, but it actually makes a lot more sense if you think about it. Now this actually ties in very well with what the "Celts" believed. There is a lot of evidence to show that the Brythonic Celts of Wales especially had this concept of the Cauldron of Cerridwen where we all go back into the cauldron when we die, and it's only the most elite and special people — who have earned the right to reincarnate as whole entities — who are able to climb out unscathed from the cauldron. Everyone else gets boiled down into the soup and recycled.

This is really an important thing for me. It's a very key part of the Tradition that I follow, the concept of the Mighty Dead. These are people who, through acts of heroism, great spirituality, military leadership, or great artistic ability or creativity, earn the right to join the ranks of the Mighty Dead. They end up becoming the great teachers, the great bards, the great characters of history and mythology. And you and I really have got a long way to go before we get there. So, its soup for us, I'm afraid. And that's not necessarily a bad thing.

The basic idea about the soup is that all these components get pulled out in different combinations, and it's, if you like, the powers that be are looking for stable combinations. And when a combination is stable, it creates the scenario where that person is able to qualify to become one of the Mighty Dead, and then they continue on.

The whole idea of this is that we often think of spiritual evolution as being something very much on an individual basis, but as far as the universe is concerned, one individual's spiritual evolution isn't that important. The most important thing is spiritual evolution of the race as a whole, the species as a whole, and so this concept of trying out the combinations and recycling gives us the best of all worlds really, because things that don't work, that aren't promoting spiritual evolution, are going to get cleaned out.

So Adolf Hitler got put back in the soup, so, we don't have to deal with his spiritual debt, as it were, from his actions polluting the over-all spirituality of the human species. However, the bits that went up to make Adolf Hitler get recombined with other pieces and maybe they come out better in the long run. And meanwhile, you have these people who are doing these great heroic or spiritual acts or great creative artists becoming eligible to reincarnate.

It's not a conscious decision on the part of some overwhelming judgmental God or anything like that. It's just a matter of when the combination of parts is stable, and you get thrown into the cauldron, the parts don't fall apart and you don't join the soup. You stay whole and complete and are able to climb out of the caldron again. It's as simple as that. It's pure and simple metaphysics. I guess that's the best way of describing it.

Now, this then enables these people who've managed to retain their integrity and come back as themselves for several lives, to be the great teachers. And their spiritual level is elevated because of their status. And they are also, through being role models and actively through teaching others, able to raise the spiritual level of other individuals. And this gradually brings the whole of humanity up to a higher level of existence. That's the theory anyway, despite the evidence that you see around you, with violence, wars, and G. W. Bush, I firmly believe that is true. The human race as a whole is becoming more spiritual, more self aware, more awakened. And this is very important, because that's what it's all about.

The really cool thing about the Cauldron and the Mighty Dead of course, is that it ties in with the mythology of Gwyn ap Nudd and the wild hunt. In most Welsh traditions, it is Gwyn ap Nudd and his wild hunt who come charging around at Samhain to collect up the souls of those who've passed away during the past year, to escort them into the mound, to Summerland, and ultimately to the Cauldron and the soup. So there you go. Now you know what's for supper.

The whole idea of karma and the "law of three", "threefold return" and all that, is not really where I'm coming from, if you haven't already figured that out by now. The important thing to remember is that all these laws are constructs, conventions to help us to understand something. And one of the biggest mistakes we can make is taking these things as literal laws of nature. The "law of three" was supposed to say that what goes around comes around. You're going to push energy out into the universe and chances are sooner or later it's going to come back and bite you on the butt.

This is why traditional Witches, cunning folk tend to work more from the concept of doing what is necessary and paying the coin, taking responsibility for your actions and being prepared to pay the price. If you're not prepared to pay the price, then don't do the deed — it's as simple as that. For us, karma isn't really a concept or term that we would use. We'd be more inclined to talk about Fate.

Fate of course is a much maligned word these days, because people tend to look at the concept of a fatalist. You know, this is the way it's going to be, this is the way it's meant to be, and you can't dodge your fate. It's like a bullet with your name on it and sooner or later it's going to catch up with you. This is not a popular way of looking at the universe. People like to look at the concept of free will and say, you know, I can do what I want. I can choose my life. I can choose to avoid certain traits within myself and to improve myself. And to a certain extent, you can, within the dictates of your fate.

This is something that on various online lists there has been huge arguments about. The idea that Fate is what dictates the way we live our lives and that the concept of free will is to a large extent an illusion. Those of us who use the concept of Fate in our world view, we often talk about the Queen of Fate.

The Queen of Fate is the mystical fourth face of the Goddess, if you like: Maid, Mother, Crone, and Queen. So we actually have four faces, because we look at things a little differently in case you hadn't guessed.

The Queen of Fate is an interesting concept because she is often seen as cold and merciless. Arianrod is the Queen of Fate in Welsh mythology, and she is seen as being quite cold and merciless, especially in the story of Llew Llaw Gyffes her son, where she cursed him with three geasa: that he will never receive a name unless it comes from her and she isn't going to give him a name (and Uncle Gwydion and Llew get around that one); And then she curses him that he will never receive arms, which means he can never be an adult unless she gives them to him and she'll never do that (and Uncle Gwydion and Llew manage to work around that one); then finally, she says that he will never have mortal bride — and Uncle Gwydion and uncle Math get together and build him a Flower Maiden so that he can have his jollies, sow his wild oats as it were. Ha, ha.

And a lot of people see Arianrhod as being this cold hearted bitch who tries her best to make his life a misery, because he showed her up by proving she wasn't a virgin, by making his arrival in the world at the moment of her being tested for her virginity. Of course, this is another case of taking things metaphorical as literal truth, and what we're really looking at is the concept that if she had just given him these things, they would have been more or less meaningless.

So she had to do what she did, he was fated to have to work for them, to earn them if you like, make them his own. And she gave him actually a very great gift; because the ultimate result of her gift to him was his own immortality and his place the constellation of Welsh deities, which of course, from my perspective are the ones who are the best. But you might disagree with that if you're not into Welsh deities.

The whole concept of free will, is it reality, illusion, or both? Well you know, there is an old tale that if you ask any two Witches for their opinion you'll get three answers, and this is very much a situation where that is the case. Free will is on the face of it, an illusion, because we are guided by Fate, and we are fated to be who we are, and to do what we do. But actually there's a lot more to it than that. Like most things in Witchcraft, the reality is a little more complex than the simplistic truth. One of the things that you have to take into account of course is that many things in Witchcraft involve the resolution of paradox, and the subject of fate and free will is no exception.

Paradox for those who didn't swallow a dictionary for breakfast is where two things are totally incompatible. An oxymoron is a phrase that is a paradox, like military intelligence, because the two just don't go together. Paradox is like traveling back in time and killing your grandfather. It creates a paradox because if you killed your grandfather, then chances are you would not have been born and therefore you could not have gone back and killed your grandfather, which means that you would have been born, which means you could have, and so on and so forth.

There are a lot of things like that in Witchcraft, paradoxes, and the trick is that when you have to reconcile two apparently opposing and incompatible things, that third thing that creates the harmony between them is the thing that is generally true. This is illustrated by the flaming lantern or flaming torch between the horns of Baphomet. And so we talk about the flaming brow of Taliesin being an example of that too. So, free will is for most people an illusion. You think you have free will, but really you're just following your predestined path.

Of course, the role of the Witch is traditionally to cheat Fate. Once again, there's a paradox there, because how to you cheat fate? You cheat it by surrendering to it, by working with it. It's almost like some of these martial arts moves, like in Aikido, where you use the strength of your enemy against him by bending and going with the flow. And this is exactly how it works, by surrendering to Fate and accepting it, you can transcend it and therefore cheat it, except it would be your Fate to transcend it, so it's not really cheating, if you see what I mean. It gets very complicated talking about it.

The best way to describe it is the way I did on an online discussion on a Yahoo list with Robin Artisson, who you may remember from the interview on the Crooked Path podcast. We were discussing Fate on the list, and there were lots of arguments to-ing and fro-ing. I finally put in my five cents worth, and it seemed to go down pretty well, so I'll share it here as well. The basic idea is that at any given instant in time — time of course being relative and a paradox all by itself — at any particular instant you are fated to react the way you react. Whatever happens right now you are going to be reacting to it totally predictably because you will react the way that you react to it. There's nothing can change that.

However, you can, with an awareness of this, gradually transform who you are in such a way that you would react differently. And so, whilst in the instant, you are bound to react as your Fate dictates, and there's no way around that, you have to bear in mind that Fate is not something that written ahead of time. There is no past, present, future. It's all a cosmic now. And so, Fate is constantly being written as you do it. So, all it's really saying is, rather than saying from the moment you were born you were destined to be hit by a bus at the age of fifteen, what it's saying is that if you don't do anything to alter who you are, then that will happen.

But, maybe on the way you become more spiritual, and you become more aware, and therefore whatever the event was that led to you stepping in front of that bus in the initial scenario, is changed. It's not a very good example, but it's about the best I can do really without waving my hands around. You being able to see me wave my hand, somehow that makes it make much more sense. But, the basic concept is, to reiterate, that whilst Fate is written in stone, it is written in stone instant by instant, and so it is only in that instant that you are bound by it

How it gets written is down to your level of awareness, your level of spirituality, your level of effort if you like. So you can actually work with Fate, surrender yourself to Fate and work within its parameters and overcome the limitations of what would have been your Fate had you not been awake and aware and a Witch, which I think is very important. So if that made any sense at all, I'd appreciate somebody letting me know, because I'm always trying to find a way to make it succinct and easy to understand.

Oaths and Pacts

Now oaths are a subject that can raise blood pressure and so on and so forth. It's a word that's associated with secret societies such as The Golden Dawn, The Freemasons, the Rosicrucian's, fraternities, and with all the negative implications that can have with some people.

The idea of swearing allegiance comes difficult for some people especially in this country, because everybody has such an independent spirit. And when you actually look historically at some of the oaths sworn by members of certain secret societies — the blood curdling oaths spelling out dire consequences for anyone who breaks them — they're enough to give you sleepless nights if you read too many of them, to be honest.

Probably the granddaddy of them all is the oath of Freemasonry which apparently includes the immortal phrase, "to have your tongue ripped out and your throat cut and your heart plucked from your chest", or something like that, anyway, really nasty, physical, murderous things to happen. Even in Wicca, the oath talks about, "and if I betray this, my solemn vow, may my weapons turn against me and may I experience that death of the soul which is absence of the presence of the Goddess" or something like that. It's been a long time since I've done a Wiccan initiation, so, I can't remember it too clearly.

But anyway, it's the idea of making hidebound promises with dire consequences for breaking them, that's really quite off-putting for some people. I know a lot of people in the general Pagan community have taken the attitude, "Why do I want to do this?" And you know, I can quite understand that. In Freemasonry and organizations such as The Golden Dawn and the Rosicrucian's, the Builders of the Adytum, and the OTO, the oaths are there to protect the secrets of the order, not because destruction will rain down upon the earth if it gets into the wrong hands, but it's more a sort of proprietary thing. It's a copyright issue as much as anything else. This is our stuff. Keep your mitts off. Of course, they don't portray it that way.

I seem to remember in Aleister Crowley's autobiography, he talks about having to take this blood curdling oath to become an initiate of The Golden Dawn, this great oath of secrecy, and as a result of taking that oath and being initiated, he is then proudly presented with the Hebrew alphabet. It's a little bit of an anti-climax, if you see what I mean. So why do secret societies have oaths? Well, unfortunately for some groups, they tend to be more a tool of control than anything else. If you have sworn an oath, you are in danger of at the very least of being kicked out of the group if you break that oath, which means that they have leverage on you. They are able to make sure that you don't talk about what goes on, so that people don't learn that it's really just a drinking club, in the case of certain fraternal organizations.

In other circumstances, maybe there are things of dubious legality going on. After all, the Freemasons are not unknown to have had their lodges used as bases to foment rebellion, not least the rebellion that resulted in this country in which we live, the good old United States. And that's a very important thing to consider. But there's also a lot of mystique associated with oaths and secret societies, and so a lot of people actually join them purely for that reason. On other occasions, you have organizations like P2 in Italy which was a major political organization within the Freemasons, not necessarily organized as part of The Freemasons. But a couple of people who were Freemasons took advantage of the oath of secrecy to set up a society within a society to undertake dubious doings of a political nature within Italy.

That became quite a scandal when people broke their oath and had the punishment part of their oath fulfilled. I believe one of them, whose name escapes me, was found killed in the classic Masonic way, according to the oath.

Of course, your average Wiccan coven isn't going to quite do that sort of stuff to you. But they are going to hold it over you if you disagree with them. Sometimes oaths can be badly misused. Luckily, I've never personally experienced that, but I have heard stories. Probably the worst way, or the most common way rather, that oaths are misused is in the case of empty promises.

An oath is normally a two way thing. You promise to keep the secrets and follow the rules and in return they actually are supposed to give you some secrets and give you some benefits of membership. And quite often, oaths are just plain not worth taking in many organizations, because you're not going to get anything of value in return. There are a lot of covens out there who will give you the traditional blood curdling oath to take upon your initiation, and there's nothing they're going to teach you that you can't find in a book for yourself. And that's really a sad state of affairs.

It's a comment on the Pagan community at large that there are an awful lot of empty shells out there unfortunately. But that's part of the process when you, a serious student who is finding out what the good sources are. And for me, the important thing is to actually think very carefully. When you come to a point where they're asking you to take an oath, if you haven't already started asking questions of yourself, now is the time to do it. You want to ask yourself, "Do I really want to bind myself to these people? Are there any red flags that tell me I shouldn't? Do I feel comfortable putting an obligation upon myself to these people, to align myself with them? Are these people whose behaviour is something that I aspire to within myself? Can I see them as role models? Is there anything that makes me nervous about this?"

Well that last one — there should always be a yes answer to that, but in this case I mean in the sense of feeling that something isn't right. You really do need to look at this.

Any organization that takes you into an initiation, and does not let you know what the oath is going to be before you have it presented to you to actually say, that is a time to walk away. You do not want to be putting yourself in the stressful and very emotional situation of an initiation and at that point, come across the oath for the first time as somebody reads it to you a line at a time for you to repeat. You need to have a copy of that oath before hand to actually read through it and make sure that you are actually willing to say it. If there's anything about sexual favours, well it's up to you whether you go ahead with that or not. But obviously anything you don't like, don't dismiss it out of hand.

Talk to the High Priest or High Priestess or Magister, or whatever the head of the group is called. And express your concerns. "You know, I'm not really happy with the way this is worded. Can you put my mind at rest?" And if they fly off the handle at that point, it's a good time to say, "Ok, I'm walking away now." But they might give you a perfectly acceptable explanation of what it means, in which case once again if you have no problem, feel free to go ahead. But don't be afraid to walk away if it doesn't feel right.

Taking an oath and joining a group just because you want to be a member of a group is not the right reason. You need to know that it's the right group for you. And you need to know, more importantly, that it's not the wrong group for you. So, take that into consideration and think very carefully before you agree to take any oath with any group. And always walk into it with your eyes at least half open.

So what about oaths in a Traditional Witchcraft Coven? Well, that's a very good question because obviously with traditional Witchcraft, you don't tend to get a lot of details about other traditions. So most of what I'm going to talk about is relevant to my own personal practice. But I think in general it applies across the board.

One of the things that I do know is that there are oaths in traditional Witchcraft. And depending on the nature of the tradition that you're following, they can be one of several types. Most groups of a traditional nature tend to talk about a rite of adoption or of fostering or of bringing into the family rather than initiation. And so the oath often reflects that. It's more of a statement of family than anything else. Also, whilst in Wicca and the ceremonial magic orders, the oaths tend to be a matter of pledging allegiance to the group and to the leader of the group, oaths within a traditional structure tend to be more of a pact between yourself and your gods, your ancestors, and so on and so forth.

There is a lot less of the "You are my fearless leader and I will follow you no matter where." Because the nature of traditionals is that they're a fairly ornery, independent bunch and they're going to follow their own path anyway. So trying to tie someone down with an oath to following somebody else's line isn't going to be very convenient or very useful.

One of the really big differences, I think, is that while the ceremonial bunch tend to be very big on making their oaths all about secrecy. You swear to keep secret their deep dark deeds. In traditional covens, you tend to talk more about silence than secrecy. Silence is not so much, never discuss these things as don't talk about them inappropriately. Silence is matter of using your intelligence and using your intuition and using your common sense to see whether it is appropriate to discuss the subject. So it's not an all out "thou shalt not talk of these things". It's more of a case of think about who you talk to. And use an appropriate level of discretion when you're doing that. So silence rather than secrecy which is, I think, a very important difference.

The first oath you're likely to be asked to take in a traditional coven is an obligation to your gods, a pact with your patron or with the deities of the tradition in general. A pact with your personal deity is most common. It really doesn't have anything at all to do with the group that you're learning with, and that's exactly the way it should be. So you're not placing yourself under any real obligation to the group. You're placing yourself under an obligation, into a relationship between you and your gods, which of course is a very serious matter, if you're taking a thorough approach to your path. But it is a significant difference. You're not kowtowing to some other human being. You're very much establishing a relationship with the deity so that you can progress on your personal path, regardless of whether you stay with the group or not. And that's the whole point.

For want of a better description, the first admission, the induction into the group for fostering is a sort of trial period that you're entering. You've probably done a year or so of training as a seeker, pre-Dedicant and Dedicant at this point, which means you're getting to the point where you're ready to start learning. So you're taken in as a fosterling to the family so that they can start to share with you the experiences that will help you to formulate your path.

And it may be that as time goes by, you discover that your path doesn't coincide with the group. So they leave it in such a way that it is perfectly ok for you to leave the group at some point when you or they discover that it's not the place you need to be. Most ethical groups will do their best to help you find a direction, your path, as you walk away from them. They tend to be very helpful that way.

Another really big difference between Wicca and traditional Witchcraft as in Wicca, everybody gets to be a High Priest or High Priestess if they want. It's very much a "if you want it, you can do it", the very Roman idea of "everybody is equal", everybody has the same rights, and if they want it, they should be allowed to have it.

In traditional Witchcraft, this is not the case. This is the narrow path. This is the road less traveled. It's the path for the few. And that's not meant in an elitist sense; it's that most people aren't not daft enough to want to walk down it. So, people start down this path for one reason or another, and discover that it isn't for them. We help them on their way to find what does work for them.

So you start off with an obligation to your gods. The next step on the way a bit later on is the obligation to your ancestors. You make a pact with your ancestors. And at this point I guess, it's more of a formal induction into the family. This is where the rite of adoption takes place. And it can be done very simply.

In my own group, we almost don't have any formal structure to this at all. We undergo an exercise during which the ancestors either accept you or not. And if they accept you, you are in and the bond is assumed and implied at that point. There is no ambiguity to it, and we don't dress it up with fancy words, but it's just simply there. Then of course, obligation to your ancestors can often be tied into an obligation to your coven or group. Not absolutely one hundred percent necessary, but it is quite common for that to be part and parcel. After all, you're forming an allegiance, forming a bond, a pact with the ancestors of the tradition, and that by definition includes the fellow members of the coven or group.

So there is that bond of support and service there as well, which in a good group is not really stressed. But it's there and it works in a very dynamic way, and the whole thing is tied up. I mentioned ethical groups. Probably oaths are the most obvious area where ethics have to be one hundred percent kosher. If a group is being unethical about their oaths, then you can pretty much guarantee that they're not going to be ethical about anything else either, and you want to run screaming from them as fast as you can. The oath is a pact. It's a business transaction. It's a two way thing. You have to remember that. No matter what the wording, it's always a two way thing.

You are making an obligation, and they are making an obligation back, whether it's the gods, the ancestors, or the people in the group. So it's very important that honour is honoured, for want of a better phrase that everybody is able to keep the word that they make. And this is one of the reasons why the grandiose statements and threats of punishment are really irrelevant, because if you break this oath you are breaking your pact with your deity, you are breaking your pact with your ancestors, you are shattering any chance you have of continuing along your personal spiritual path for this lifetime.

And so, really you bring about the punishment on yourself rather anybody else having to impose it on you, and that's why oaths in this kind of group tend not to include the blood curdling punishment, because they're not needed. If you screw up, break your oath, become a warlock, you're fucked anyway. You're not going to get anywhere by doing that, because you cut yourself off from the gods, you cut yourself off from the ancestors. What is left of your path to follow? Because they're so bound up with each other, you cannot follow the path without the gods, without the ancestors. By whatever way you perceive them, they are part and parcel of the path. And so cutting yourself off from where you're meant to be is actually a very terrible punishment and you do it to yourself. So, remember that.

Initiation

What are we talking about when we use the term initiation? Now the word literally means a beginning, a start of something. And this is probably one of the biggest areas of contention because most people seem to work towards initiation as if it were a goal, it was the end of the journey, when in actual fact, it should be considered the first step on the journey.

We always tell our initiates, once they've been initiated, that now they really start to learn, because really everything leading up to that point was just preparing them for the experience of initiation. Of course, there are several different things that come under the category of initiation when we're talking about magical groups, and we're going to start off by taking a look at the initiation ritual as a rite of passage.

Initiation into the group, this is often a very key moment in anybody's studies, because it's the point at which you cease to be a 'maybe' member of the group and become an actual member of the group. It's the point at which you start to really start learning the inner workings of the tradition that you're studying, and so this is very, very key, but does it have any significance beyond that?

Well, for starters it is a rite of passage, and rites of passage for many reasons, psychological, social, even physiological in some respects can have quite a profound effect on us. Other rites of passage are of course, there's the ultimate rites of passage of birth and death, which are really take you from one world into another in a very literal way.

And then there's the naming rite, by whatever name your spiritual path uses, Christening, Wiccaning, so on and so forth — the rite of adulthood, of coming of age. A wedding is a rite of passage into a new state of existence as part of a couple, and divorce as well can be a rite of passage, especially if you have a nasty one.

But all these rites of passage come from community life, and they tend to have a very profound effect on us psychologically. A rite of initiation into a group, a magical group, coven, whatever you want to call it, is no less profound in a psychological sense, because it is a sort of coming of age, becoming a valid member of society type thing within this very specialized group. You're no longer seen as children. You're seen people who are responsible and ready to learn the secrets, if you like.

It all sounds very mysterious, learning deep dark secrets of the tradition, and it usually turns out to be a little disappointing if you think about it in that sense. Remember one of the great quotes about Aleister Crowley was how he, at his Golden Dawn initiation, swore these huge oaths of secrecy, never to reveal what was given to him within the confines of the temple, and they then presented to him the great secret of the Hebrew alphabet, which he wasn't overly impressed with.

This is one of the issues that a lot of groups come up against time and time again, this anticlimactic nature of some of the rituals. My own experience, having been something of a initiation whore, I've joined lots of different groups over the years, ceremonial magic, Wiccan, traditional witchcraft, and one of the things a lot of them have in common is that the initiation ritual starts out as being this mysterious thing that "how am I going to survive it?" and by the end of it, you're sort of "oh, will it please end before I die of boredom?"

Especially in ceremonial groups, the symbolism is laid on so thick that it obscures any real sort of participation on the part of the initiate.

The candidate is moved from point to point and has symbol after symbol thrown at them and it all becomes a meaningless daze after a while. You have to wonder whether there was really any point to it in the first place by the time you get to the end. A lot of the ceremonial groups follow the format of Masonic initiations which are big on symbolism. Of course, one of the advantages the Masons have is that their initiation has a few very key points to it that makes it very effective psychologically, and unfortunately, they tend to be the things that get left out by magical groups. So you end up with the words and the movements and the symbolism, and it can be very moving, but there's always that danger of slipping into role playing, which really doesn't do a lot of good.

And when you rely on a symbolic initiation ritual, there is always that danger, because there isn't really any way you can fail initiations based on symbolism, unless there's a test, and very rarely is there a test that they're going to fail. So the most important thing about the rite of passage that is initiating into a group is the act of joining the family or the tradition. Whilst this can be a very magically effective experience as I'll discuss shortly, for the most part it tends to be something along the lines of fraternity initiations, often complete with hazing and joshing about and trying to terrify the poor candidate beforehand as well. You know, that's a fine old tradition too, but it's not really an essential part of the experience.

Now sometimes groups do, do something a bit more profound, and most often the most profound initiations, rites of passage into a group, are the ones where there is some reciprocal accepting going on. It's not just the person being inducted into the group, but the group being wrapped around the person. And the most significant of all is where there is some sort of claiming of the candidate by the group, and this is often done in traditional witchcraft, it's often the ancestors that do the claiming in some from or other.

Many of the groups that refer to themselves as family traditions or even just traditional witchcraft groups these days, will tend to have a two tier sort of passage of entry. The first is a rite of fostering, where you get to become a formal student. You're an initiate student, but you're not full family, you've been fostered rather than made a member of the family.

Then later on there is a rite of adoption, which is the being claimed by the ancestors and the gods of the tradition. And this can be very, very profound, both on the psychological level and also on the magical level. This is where it starts to get really interesting. It's one of the things that we do in our own group. I mean, I don't think there's any secrets being given away, because there isn't really any secret to it. We have that two tier approach and it's not so much a case of somebody being more important or more in the group if they've taking the second part of the thing. It's just a matter of you get initiated into our group, you get fostered in and you become a crafter, and at some point you reach a level of experience and hunger as much as anything else that you decide to take that next step and that next step is to go through a process where you are claimed by the ancestors. And it's a very simple, they either claim you or they don't. It's very unambiguous. And it's been very effective for us.

And there's no pomp and circumstance with us. We don't do big drawn out rituals for this. It's just a particular experience that either does or does not succeed for you. And that's it, end of story. The first initiation is very big on some other aspects, and I'll be talking about some of that later, because that ties in more with the inner initiation, which is the other side of the coin, and which is really the most important one.

So, the rite of passage into the group is very important psychologically as a way of making you feel like you belong to the group and feel united and an integral part of it and very much important. The traditional witch is the aspect of being claimed by the tradition, by the ancestors, but the ultimate initiatory experience is one that cannot be given to you by any tradition. It may occur within the practices of a tradition, but ultimately it occurs within you. And this is the personal inner initiation.

So the real initiation, which comes from within, it's the initiation that we're all talking about when we actually talk about initiation, it's the big one. It is the direct experience between you and your path, your spirituality, your deities, however you want express it, but the most important thing is that it comes from within and it comes from you. There's nobody that can give it to you or bestow it upon you or make it happen for you.

In an ideal situation, a teacher or a group that you're working with will provide you with experiences that will facilitate the development of a state of existence within you where you can encounter the true initiation, and if you're really lucky, this will coincide with some sort of rite of passage initiatory experience within the group. That's what we usually try to aim for in my group, is to try and get the candidate into a position where they're ripe for a real initiatory experience about the same time as when we do the rite of initiation into the group, so that the two more or less overlap and they can have a very profound interaction with each other in that way.

But there's no guarantees, and they don't have to coincide to be effective, each in their own sphere of existence. As I said, the most important thing to bear in mind is that this initiation comes from within you. So it's not something that is a gift given by anybody else. It's not going to be something that happens without you putting some effort into it, because it is very dependent on you actually being ready for it, and this is what a lot of the training in a good group is all about, is giving you the tools and giving you the experiences to get yourself into a place where you can enter that fulcrum point at the heart of the compass where everything is now and everything is one, where you can encounter the experiences that transform you.

This is what initiation is about. It's about inner transformation. Once you've experienced an inner initiation, you will never be the same again, and this is probably one of the biggest differences between the group initiation and the inner initiation, is that you can leave a group but you can never walk away from an initiation that happened at an inner level. It's part and parcel of you. It's literally part of your DNA. There's no going back, no turning back the clock to before it, and this can be enough reason for people to say, "No, I'm done." They catch a glimpse of what's around the corner, realize that if they take that extra step, that what they're glimpsing is going to be part and parcel of their lives from there onwards, and they decide not to take that step. That is a perfectly valid choice to make, and that is in and of itself a form of initiation, although it's an initiation into a more mundane way of being, because you've turned away from what might have been.

And you know, they're not always easy. There are — you know it's not like there's just one big one — a series of these that go on for the rest of your life essentially. But the important thing here, I think, is that you very much get a hunger for this, and it's the needing to step forward into that darkness and accept the experience for what it is that makes it a very profound experience for you. As I said, that once you've taken that step there is no going back, and it does tend to change your life in every aspect. The mundane, the spiritual, your interactions with other people, it does tend to have very profound effects, and people do notice.

We talk about the Witch's Mark or the Mark of Cain, which is the mark of the initiate, and some groups actually physically mark their initiates and some groups don't, but everyone who undergoes one of these inner initiations is marked in a way that is very clear to others who have also been through these experiences. You can always tell another initiate without being told, because you can see the scars if you like of that initiation upon their psyche. You can see the mark on their aura.

You can see, you can just tell, because something in you resonates with them and you realize that you are talking to a kindred spirit. And that is really quite an amazing thing when you get that. When you get a group that is very good at bringing people to these points of inner initiation, and so that you have the majority of the members of the group do actually undergo these inner initiations, they tend to become very close knit.

They tend to become very good at communicating with each other about these things, which is in itself very rare, because communicating these inner experiences is very difficult, because finding words for it is very hard. But when you're speaking to someone who's already been through it, you find you can communicate it better, because the few words that are available tend to work that much more effectively. You tend to end up with, "You remember when you do that?", "Oh yeah, I remember that." You get conversations like that. It doesn't sound like much in the way of communication, but because you've been through that shared experience, it's enough. It's enough to trigger what you're getting, what you're trying to get across, and this is really quite a profound part of the bond that initiates share.

It's a very powerful compensation for the other part of the... you know... the curse, if you like, of the inner initiation, which is the isolation that it places upon you, because these initiations, these inner initiations are very personal and very intimate. They're also very isolating. I talked in the pilot episode of this podcast about the terrible loneliness of the initiate, the sense of wandering in the wasteland alone, even when you're part of a group. You get these very profound moments of realizing that though you walk alongside others, you are in fact isolated and completely alone, and this can be very difficult to deal with.

It's one of the things that people can shy away from, and that prevents people from going further into the mysteries. But that is as it should be, because it's not meant to be for everybody to walk through these mysteries. It's meant for the few people to take the road less traveled and to do what they can to grow spiritually and promote themselves through these experiences in the hopes that by doing so they gradually help the human race to do the same, by pulling itself up by its own bootstraps.

This has often been described as the great work. It's the idea of the individual striving for their own personal spiritual evolution, by doing so helps to raise the evolutionary state of the entire human race. And so, whether we like it or not, the human race as a whole gradually becomes more spiritual. Despite the evidence to the contrary that we see in the world around us, there is evidence to suggest that the human race is becoming more spiritual.

Part of the process is becoming more self aware, and this is the status that we find ourselves in now where the... this going to sound terribly old fashioned and I apologize if it offends anyone, but I'm just putting forward a theoretical principle here, the idea that historically the human race has not been really known for individuality. In medieval times the feudal mindset was the way things went, and everybody worked together in a sort of communal way. Individuality was not rewarded and not expected.

As time has passed by, the great individuals have cropped up, individual thinkers like Galileo and Newton and so on and so forth, all great thinkers and philosophers and inventors and scientists, and gradually the concept of individuality has become more of a reality for the human race. Now what we find is that the western world has become very self absorbed, because we've become very aware of ourselves, and we're going through a phase that is akin to the teenage years, I guess, in human terms, because we've become self aware and so self is all we are aware of at the moment.

The third world countries, some of them have retained that group mentality for longer. And so they're starting to develop this self awareness and they're starting to make a little noise about that. And so what you see is an interesting mix in the world now, where the various states of spiritual evolution are coming into conflict, because everything has its native aspects.

You sort of go through a negative process when you achieve self awareness, because you become self absorbed, you become very childish and selfish and wanting everything for yourself, and it takes a little while for that to settle in and for you to start to actually look at things from a wider perspective and let the self awareness stop being a negative and start being positive thing, enables you to actually operate for the greater good. So I think there's a lot of promise for the human race as long as we keep on evolving spiritually.

Bibliography

Peter Paddon

The Crooked Path: Selected Transcripts (2009) Pendraig Publishing, Los Angeles

The Book of the Veil (1995) Capall Bann, London

Through the Veil (1996) Capall Bann, London

Nigel Jackson

Masks of Misrule (1996) Capall Bann, London

The Call of the Horned Piper (2001) Capall Bann, London

Nigel Pennick

Practical Magic in the Northern Tradition (2005) Thoth Publications, London

Secrets of East Anglian Magic (2005) Holmes Publishing Group, London

Natural Magic (2005) Lear Books, London

Crossing the Borderlines (1998) Capall Bann, London

Gwyn

Light From the Shadows (2000) Capall Bann, London

Nigel Pearson
Treading the Mill (2007) Capall Bann, London

Sioned Davies
The Mabinogion (2008) Oxford University Press, USA

F. Marian McNeill
The Silver Bough Vols. 1 – 4 (1977) William MacLellan Stuart, Edinburgh

Robin Artisson
The Horn of Evenwood (2007) Pendraig Publishing, Los Angeles
The Flaming Circle (2008) Pendraig Publishing, Los Angeles
Witching Way of the Hollow Hill (2009) Pendraig Publishing, Los Angeles

Radomir Ristic
Balkan Traditional Witchcraft (2009) Trans. Michael Carter, Pendraig Publishing, Los Angeles

C. R. Bilardi
The Red Church or the Art of Pennsylvania German Braucherei (2009) Pendraig Publishing, Los Angeles

Index

A

B

C

D

E

F

G

H

I

J

K

L

M

N

O

P

Q

R

S

T

U

V

W

Y

About the Author

Peter is a Brit of Welsh ancestry who lives in Los Angeles with his wife Linda, where he is Magister of Briar Rose, a small Coven of modern Cunningfolk. Aside from being an author, Peter also created the Craftwise series of spellcasting DVDs, and is the host of the Crooked Path podcast.

Having many years of experience in various forms of Occult Studies, including Alexandrian Wicca, the Egyptian Mysteries, Rosicrucianism and Enochian magick, Peter finally found what he had been looking for all his life in the two Traditional Covens he became a member of in the US. The first was the Roebuck (1734, Clan of Tubal Cain), under Ann and Dave Finnin, and the second was Wildewood Grove (Welsh Celtic Tradition), under its Mistress, Raven Womack.

More Magickal Works from Pendraig Publishing

Balkan Traditional Witchcraft
Radomir Ristic

Buckland's Domino Divinaton
Fortune-Telling with Döminös and the Games of Döminös
Raymond Buckland

Buckland's Practical Color Magick
Raymond Buckland

Hedge-Rider
Witches and the Underworld
Eric De Vries

Magical Rites from the Crystal Well
The Classic Book for Witches and Pagans
Ed Fitch

Masks of the Muse
Building a relationship with the Goddess of the West
Veronica Cummer

Mastering the Mystical Heptarchy
Scott Stenwick

Scottish Herbs and Fairy Lore
Ellen Evert Hopman

Sorgitzak: Old Forest Craft
Stories and messages
from the gods of Old Europe
Veronica Cummer

Sybil Leek:
Out of the Shadows
Christine Jones

The Crooked Path
Selected Transcripts from
the Crooked Path Podcast
Peter Paddon

The Flaming Circle
A Reconstruction of the
Old Ways of Britain and Ireland
Robin Artisson

The Forge of Tubal Cain
Southern California Witchcraft,
Roebuck, and the Clan of Tubal Cain
Ann Finnin

The Horn of Evenwood
Robin Artisson

The Resurrection of the Meadow
Robin Artisson

To Fly By Night
An Anthology of Hedgewitchery
Veronica Cummer

Visceral Magick
Bridging the Gap
Between Magic and Mundane
Peter Paddon

Witching Way of the Hollow Hill
The Gramarye of the Folk
Who Dwell Below the Mound
Robin Artisson

9418073R10095

Printed in Great Britain
by Amazon.co.uk, Ltd.,
Marston Gate.